Nations in the News

IRAN

Afghanistan

China

India

Iran

The Koreas

Mexico

Russia

Saudi Arabia

Syria

United Kingdom

Nations in the News
IRAN

BY Norm Geddis

MASON CREST
Philadelphia · Miami

Mason Crest
450 Parkway Drive, Suite D
Broomall, PA 19008
(866) MCP-BOOK (toll free)
www.masoncrest.com

Copyright © 2020 by Mason Crest, an imprint of National Highlights, Inc. All rights reserved. No part of this publication may be reproduced or transmitted in any form or by any means, electronic or mechanical, including photocopying, recording, taping, or any information storage and retrieval system, without permission in writing from the publisher.

Printed in the United States of America.

First printing
9 8 7 6 5 4 3 2 1

Series ISBN: 978-1-4222-4242-1
Hardcover ISBN: 978-1-4222-4246-9
ebook ISBN: 978-1-4222-7574-0

Cataloging-in-Publication Data is available on file at the Library of Congress.

Developed and Produced by Print Matters Productions, Inc. (www.printmattersinc.com)

Cover and Interior Design by Tom Carling, Carling Design Inc.

Contents

KEY ICONS TO LOOK FOR

Words to Understand: These words with their easy-to-understand definitions will increase the reader's understanding of the text while building vocabulary skills.

Sidebars: This boxed material within the main text allows readers to build knowledge, gain insights, explore possibilities, and broaden their perspectives by weaving together additional information to provide realistic and holistic perspectives.

Educational Videos: Readers can view videos by scanning our QR codes, providing them with additional educational content to supplement the text.

Text-Dependent Questions: These questions send the reader back to the text for more careful attention to the evidence presented there.

Research Projects: Readers are pointed toward areas of further inquiry connected to each chapter. Suggestions are provided for projects that encourage deeper research and analysis.

Series Glossary of Key Terms: This back-of-the-book glossary contains terminology used throughout this series. Words found here increase the reader's ability to read and comprehend higher-level books and articles in this field.

The ruins of Persepolis, an ancient Persian capital, were constructed 2,500 years ago.

Iran at a Glance

Total Land Area	636,371 square miles
Climate	Mostly arid or semiarid; subtropical along Caspian coast
Natural Resources	Petroleum, natural gas, coal, chromium, copper, iron ore, lead, manganese, zinc, sulfur
Land Use	Agricultural land: 30.1 percent (10.8 percent arable land, 1.2 percent permanent crops, 18.1 percent permanent pasture); forest 6.8 percent; other 63.1 percent
Urban Population	74.9 percent of total population
Major Urban Areas	Tehran (8.896 million), Mashhad (3.097 million), Esfahan (2.041 million), Shiraz (1.605 million), Karaj (1.585 million), Tabriz (1.582 million)
Geography	Middle East, bordering the Gulf of Oman, the Persian Gulf, and the Caspian Sea, between Iraq and Pakistan

Introduction

Some nations feel they are destined for greatness. They look at the resources they have and what they've accomplished in their history and figure it adds up to something more than their neighbors, maybe more than any other country. Iran is one such nation. Many of its leaders feel they have a divine right to dominate other nations, undermine existing governments, and spread their religious form of government to other Middle Eastern countries.

These leaders have good reason to feel that Iran can be a major player on the world stage. Several times throughout its history, Iran has held together a vast and powerful empire. The country has world-superpower potential today because of its wealth of natural resources.

Other nations have experienced the same kind of wish for dominance. The United States promoted itself in the last decades of the nineteenth century as being destined for top-dog status in the twentieth century. It was right. Like the United States, Iran is a country that believes it deserves to be a world power. Today, Iran asserts its ambition and divine right at a time when U.S. **hegemony** is being challenged from multiple directions.

Words to Understand

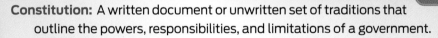

Constitution: A written document or unwritten set of traditions that outline the powers, responsibilities, and limitations of a government.

Hegemony: Dominance of one nation over others.

Sanctions: Penalties, usually of an economic nature, imposed on one country by another.

Shi'a Islam: A branch of Islam that developed in the early years of the religion; its central disagreement with Sunni Islam, the other major branch, is over the rightful successor to the prophet Muhammad.

Supreme leader: The constitutional head of state of Iran; the position is for life and is almost limitless in its power.

All the things that make up a world power are available in Iran: an abundance of good land, an educated population, a strong manufacturing output, and an experienced military. However, Iran is a country with a foot in two different worlds. It wants to be a major player in the world economy. But many of its leaders put a centuries-old interpretation of Islamic law before the country's economic interests. This slows economic progress and makes some social progress near impossible, which has made Iran isolated and perplexing to other nations.

The United States, Russia, China, the European Union, and India look at Iran as a potential problem. Certainly, the country's unclear policy on nuclear weapons has made it second only to North Korea on the worry list. North Korea and Iran are two nations that cause sleepless nights for many world leaders.

The thinking in the United States is that if Iran produces nuclear weapons, nuclear war is more likely. The United States gives many reasons for this. One is that other countries in the region would be pressured to make their own bombs. Saudi Arabia would be an example of a country tempted to go the nuclear route if Iran does. With more nuclear weapons around, accidents will be more likely. A nuclear explosion can destroy an entire city, and nuclear war could destroy the entire planet. For this reason the United States

Boxes of missiles and other weapons from Iran aboard a cargo ship intended for the Hezbollah terror organization.

uses its influence around the world to stop the spread of nuclear weapons—though some countries, including Iran, see this as hypocritical because the United States continues to build up its own military and nuclear capabilities.

Iran has resisted this outside influence. If the stakes for peace and happiness in Iran were not so high, the frequency and manner in which Iran scorns input from the United States (and vice versa) might be almost comical. At the present, however, the ugly exchanges between the United States and Iran are disturbing. The U.S. president Donald Trump tweets offhandedly about using military force against Iran, while members of the Iranian parliament burn the U.S. flag. Both sides degrade themselves out of anger.

Since the current government took power in 1979, the Iranian leaders have framed themselves as heroes fighting against a United States that supported an Iranian dictator. Iran is correct: The United States supported the pre-1979 government led by the shah of Iran. He was a dictator, and the United States continued to back him even while knowing he was oppressing and killing his own people. The government of Iran sees itself as the world's most successful "dissident" opposing U.S. world influence. The government also sees itself as empowered by adherence to religious tradition.

Iranians burn the American flag.

The vast majority of Iranians practice a form of religion that is called **Shi'a Islam**. Shi'a is one of two major branches of Islam, the other being Sunni. Iran is unique in that its population is overwhelmingly Shi'a. Most other Middle Eastern countries are dominated by Sunnis.

Iran's postrevolutionary government bound itself to an interpretation of Islamic law called *Sharia*. Sharia law is seen as inseparable from government. This has created a government like no other. Bound to serve and protect its people through direct inspiration from God, the Iranian government has passed laws that aim to protect people spiritually and economically. The reality is more complex. Some laws with good intentions have been corrupted when put into effect. Religion has been used to negate popular laws and even imprison people.

Iran's government harnesses and imprisons those who disagree with its specific kind of religious-based government. No one who criticizes it is safe, not even powerful people. Members of the government may hold prominent posts one day and find themselves under house arrest the next for saying something too critical.

But not all thought is oppressed. Great educational institutions go with great empires, and the tradition continues in Iran, even after the old empires have faded. This gives Iran an upper hand in

Each year, Iranians take to the streets to celebrate the Iranian Revolution of 1979.

In addition to the sanctions in place, Iran is on the list of countries whose citizens are banned from coming into the United States, although student visas may be granted.

a region otherwise primarily driven by oil. Iran has a "brain trust," a segment of society that can build things and empower new technologies. That said, many of those educated people are unemployed because of economic problems caused by mismanagement. Because of Iran's nuclear policy, many countries have imposed sanctions, which prevent certain goods and services from being sold to Iran. This has had a negative effect on employment as well.

Sanctions imposed by the United States and other countries have impacted many other aspects of Iranian life, including the availability of medical care. The lack of access to certain materials has meant hardship for Iranians just trying to have a career, a family, and a dignified life. Whether the "hardline" approach of the older establishment, with its strict adherence to religious tradition,

Protests in Iran

The Iranian economy has been stifled by sanctions. The stagnation and lack of opportunity has fueled recent protests. Throughout the winter of 2017 and into 2018, many street protests took place in Iran. They lasted days and even weeks in some cities. Although large protests have happened before in Iran, these were the first where activists dared criticize the religious nature of the government. Protesters directly attacked religious institutions for the first time in the summer of 2018. "Down with the dictator!" became their rallying cry as they criticized the country's powerful **supreme leader**.

will maintain its hold on the hearts and minds of average Iranians seems in doubt.

Today Iran is driven by the efforts, talents, experiences, and insights of workers whose average age is 31. The ambitions that these young Iranians have for their country seem more and more at odds with the goals of the government. U.S. sanctions threaten the well-being of all Iranians. Goods and services that are needed to create important business and infrastructure projects are prohibited. It's as though Iran's progress has come to a halt while everyone who keeps the country running waits either for the United States to change its demands or for the Iranian government to satisfy the U.S. demands for access to and accountability of Iranian nuclear activity. Moving away from any appearance of working on nuclear weapons would likely end U.S. sanctions. Even in the short time that U.S. sanctions were lifted, Iranian economic activity heated up, and residents started to breathe more easily. Offering its people a better lifestyle would go a long way to easing social tension in Iran.

In practice, the government of Iran has a guaranteed hold on power. Drastic, citizen-based reform is near impossible. For example, the **constitution** makes Islam central to the rights and operation of the government. The religious compatibility of a law must be voted on before the law can take effect. This means that making a change such as diminishing the influence of religious scholars is very unlikely.

Young people in Iran.

Islam is the center of Iranian life and law.

The Iranian government tries to keep itself in favor with working Iranians by creating ambitious social and economic projects. Some projects have worked well; others have resulted in unfinished buildings covering several city blocks. Iran has one of the most advanced health-care systems in the region. Free K–12 education is offered to every Iranian. However, economic pressures take many young people around 15 years old out of school and into the workplace.

Although the government relies heavily on its oil exports, the country has several other significant exports, like saffron. Saffron is the most expensive spice in the world. In contrast, Iran must import many of its basic foods, though the country has plenty of unused farmland.

A teenager has left K–12 education to work in a marketplace.

Iran is a complex society with a unique form of government. With its vast amount of available resources, its future is full of options. Iran could be its own obstacle in determining whether it grows economically and in terms of its political influence. It has been powerful many times in the past, and its history offers a vision of the future in which it could be one of the world's most powerful countries again.

Text-Dependent Questions

1. How do world powers tend to perceive Iran?

2. How does Iran view its relationship with the United States?

3. Name one cause of the protests that happened in Iran in 2018.

Research Project

If you are a young adult in Iran with an education, what social and economic obstacles interfere with beginning a professional career? Research stories of contemporary Iranians through magazine articles, newspaper reports, or other media. Make a list of at least five things that make starting a career difficult in Iranian society, with brief descriptions of each challenge.

Iran in the News in the 21ˢᵗ Century

Trump Abandons Iran Nuclear Deal He Long Scorned
New York Times, May 8, 2018

Iranians Take to Streets of Tehran in Biggest Protests Since 2012
The Independent, June 26, 2018

Iran Says It Plans to Boost Ballistic, Cruise Missile Capacity
Reuters, September 1, 2018

Rouhani Secures Second Term with Landslide Victory
Tehran Times, May 20, 2017

Post-Sanctions Environment Exhibition Kicks Off in Tehran
Tehran Times, March 1, 2016

Deal Reached on Iran Nuclear Program; Limits on Fuel Would Lessen with Time
New York Times, July 14, 2015

Iran's Oil Revenues Drop 58 Percent since 2011 as Sanctions Bite: U.S.
Reuters, August 30, 2013

Violence and Protest in Iran as Currency Drops in Value
New York Times, October 3, 2012

Obama Signs Iran Sanctions Bill into Law
BBC, December 31, 2011

Iran Uprising Turns Bloody
The Guardian, June 15, 2009

CHAPTER 1

Security Issues

At different times in its history, Iran has been a conqueror and a world power. During other times, it has been conquered by outsiders. The country's rich history manifests itself today as both fervent commitment and opposition to its **theocratic** government. While the government of Iran limits freedoms of the press and political parties, and often exercises brutal oppression against "illegal" opposition, a robust coalition of groups continues to fight for reform of the theocratic government. The two largest groups, the People's Mojahedin Organization of Iran (PMOI/MEK) and the National Council of Resistance of Iran (NCRI), organize protests both inside and outside of the country. Over 100,000 people filled the streets of Paris in 2016 to protest the government's oppressive tactics. They called for political freedom and democratic reforms.

Yet the current government is not without its internal and external support. The Iranian military helps like-minded countries and terrorists get weapons, resources, and training. The government makes special efforts to help groups that attack its adversary Israel.

Words to Understand

Autocrat: A ruler with absolute power.

Coup: A quick change in government leadership without a legal basis, most often by violent means.

Theocratic: Of or relating to a theocracy, a form of government that lays claim to God as the source and justification of its authority.

A demonstration by the People's Mojahedin Organization of Iran.

Iran's Security Issues at a Glance

Military Size	913,000 total personnel
Military Service	18 years of age for compulsory service; 16 years of age to volunteer; 17 years of age for entry into law enforcement; 15 years of age for entry into Basij Forces (Popular Mobilization Army); conscript military service obligation is 18 months; women exempt from military service
Military Branches	Islamic Republic of Iran Regular Forces (Artesh): Ground Forces, Navy, Air Force (IRIAF), Khatam al-Anbiya Air Defense Headquarters; Islamic Revolutionary Guard Corps (Sepâh-e Pâsdârân-e Enghelâb-e Eslâmi, IRGC): Ground Resistance Forces, Navy, Aerospace Force, Qods Force (special operations); Law Enforcement Forces (2015)
Military Spending	$14.08 billion USD (2017); 2.69 percent of GDP (2015)
Active Terrorist Groups (home-based)	Jaysh al-Adl
Active Terrorist Groups (international)	al-Qaeda, Kurdistan Workers' Party
Illicit Drugs	One of the primary transshipment routes for Southwest Asian heroin to Europe; suffers one of the highest opiate addiction rates in the world and has an increasing problem with synthetic drugs; regularly enforces the death penalty for drug offenses

Israeli naval forces guard weapons found on board a cargo ship. Iranian military forces help terror organizations, like Hezbollah, gain access to weapons like these.

Iran is a modern society. It has many of the same problems as nations in Europe and North America. Iran has the largest number of opiate addicts in the world; it both battles and sometimes helps human traffickers. Its military is known for its alliances with different criminal and terrorist organizations that are known to finance their activities through illicit human and drug trafficking. In 2011, the Iranian military sought the help of Mexican drug cartels in a plot to assassinate the Saudi ambassador in Washington, D.C. The plot failed, and a used car salesman from Texas, whose cousin was in the elite Iranian Revolutionary Guard, was sentenced to 25 years in federal prison for his participation in the scheme.

The United States looms large as Iran's biggest adversary. Since the Islamic Revolution of 1979, Iran has been a modern theocratic state. Its government has, at times, referred to the United States as the "Great Satan." Before 1979, Iran was ruled by the U.S.-supported **autocrat** called the shah of Iran, and Iran sees the United States as

an adversary because of its support for this pre-1979 government. These tensions are one of the reasons why the United States worries about Iran developing nuclear weapons. Iran supports countries around the world that also have anti-U.S. feelings, including Venezuela and Syria.

Conflicts

Iran has experienced many wars and conflicts in its 2,500-year history. In the modern era, the Iran-Iraq War has been the country's most devastating conflict.

The Iranian government that had been set up after World War II collapsed in 1979. The country's transition to its current government became known as the Islamic Revolution. It led to Iran's current status as a theocratic state.

Iran's neighbor Iraq feared the revolution might spread across the region. Iraq invaded Iran on September 22, 1980, to end the

Armed Iranian rebels fight with firearms during the Islamic Revolution in 1979.

revolution. Iran looked like an easy conquest. Iraq had more soldiers, tanks, and planes. In the early months of the war, the Iraqi army handily defeated their Iranian counterparts. But Iran then sent waves of unarmed humans at the Iraqi army. By doing this, Iran managed to put Iraq in a stalemate situation that lasted close to eight years. The Iran-Iraq War continued throughout most of the 1980s and set the tone for Iranian international relations for the next four decades. The United States provided economic aid and intelligence to the Iraqis during the war.

More than 1.5 million Iranian soldiers and civilians died in the Iran-Iraq War. An entire generation of Iranian men is said to have been lost. The war finally came to an end on August 20, 1988, after Iran and Iraq signed a United Nations–brokered settlement.

Find out what happened in the Iran-Iraq War.

Helicopter Battles

The Iran-Iraq War has the unique distinction of being the only war to have seen confirmed air-to-air helicopter battles. The Iraqi military had Soviet Mi-25s flying against Iran's American-made AH-1J SeaCobras. The SeaCobras had been sold to the shah's government prior to the Islamic Revolution. Six battles took place between 1982 and 1987. Because the SeaCobras could turn in a tighter space, they largely dominated the battles. The Iraqis saw their helicopter force dwindle from 350 helicopters to between 70 and 90 at the end of the war.

An injured Iranian soldier holds his IV bag during the Iran-Iraq War.

Iran's Military Ambitions

After the Islamic Revolution, the new government and Ayatollah Khomeini, the first supreme leader of Iran, took a more aggressive approach with the military. They created the Iranian Revolutionary Guard, which is still in existence today. One of its responsibilities is to promote other Islamic rebellions around the world. It does this by offering training, weapons, and soldiers to friendly terrorist groups.

Iran's quest for nuclear weapons did not begin after the 1979 Islamic Revolution; it preceded it. The shah, or ruling monarch of Iran, saw nuclear weapons as the means for the country to regain its long-lost dominance in the world.

During the decade after the Islamic Revolution, however, Iran had no nuclear ambition. Ayatollah Khomeini felt that nuclear weapons were too American. The next, and current, supreme leader, Ayatollah Khamenei, revived the country's interest in things nuclear. He restarted a program that on the surface works toward nuclear power. Yet this power generation program may be a front for a nuclear weapons program.

Forty years after the revolution, portraits of Ayatollah Khomeini can still be found throughout cities of Iran.

Imam Khomeini (peace be upon his soul)
The great founder of Islamic Republic of Iran

Iran Nuclear Deal

To calm world tensions surrounding Iran's possible development of nuclear weapons, Iran, the United States, the European Union, and China formed the Joint Comprehensive Plan of Action in 2015. This plan limited three important aspects of Iran's nuclear power program related to the possibility of using nuclear fuel to build nuclear weapons. Iran's stockpile of low-enriched uranium (nuclear fuel that could be used for weapons) was reduced by 97 percent. Further enrichment could be done only at a lower level not capable of producing a nuclear explosion. This part of the agreement is to last 15 years. For 10 years, Iran will put its nuclear centrifuges, devices used to enrich uranium, into storage.

In exchange, sanctions that had been crippling the Iranian economy were lifted. However, the United States unilaterally pulled out of the agreement in May of 2018. This act renewed U.S. sanctions against Iran and sent the Iranian economy into crisis. In late July of 2018, Iran's currency, the rial, lost 18 percent of its value in two days, something Iran attributed "mainly to enemies."

Iran-Israel Proxy War

Iran provides support that goes to groups seeking to attack, or even end, the state of Israel. Most of the money and guns that flow to terrorist groups like Hezbollah come from Iran. Hezbollah is a terrorist group based in Lebanon whose aim is to unite Shi'ite Islamist groups. It was originally organized with help from Iran's elite military unit, the Revolutionary Guard. Hezbollah seeks to promote Iranian-style Islamic revolution in other countries in the region, most successfully in Lebanon; its stated goals include kicking all Americans and Europeans out of Lebanon. Hezbollah garners support much like other radical groups, through hateful actions and demonizing outsiders. Israel is a perennial enemy. Hezbollah is one of several allied groups that carries out terrorist attacks and missile launches against the Jewish state.

Alliances

Russia is Iran's primary ally. Other allies include Iraq, Lebanon, Syria, the Palestinian Authority, Serbia, and Venezuela.

Iran develops its alliances in the aim of forwarding three goals: the furtherance of Shi'ite-dominated governments in the Middle East, the weakening of influence in the region enjoyed by the United States, and the weakening, if not the destruction, of Israel. To this end, Iran keeps close relationships with both Shi'ite and Sunni groups opposed to Israel. It also supports countries and organizations fighting Sunni-dominated nations like Saudi Arabia.

Iran enjoys close relations with Venezuela. This alliance has grown out of anti-U.S. sentiment. Both countries work together to help smaller nations resist U.S. hegemony. They provide loans and support where the effect will most diminish the influence of the United States. In recent decades, Russia and Iran have developed close relations based on similar anti-U.S. feelings.

Regional Relations

Iran's strongest international ties are to other states with large Muslim populations. The Iranian agency in charge of international relations is called the Ministry of Foreign Affairs. The agency is headed by the minister of foreign affairs. The minister works for the Iranian president and the supreme leader.

Russia's president, Vladimir Putin, and Iran's supreme leader, Ali Khamenei speak with one another during a state visit to Tehran.

Regional organizations like the Organization of Islamic Cooperation and the Arab Gulf Cooperation Council receive support and active participation from Iran. Iran is also involved in what is called the Non-Aligned Movement. During the Cold War of the late twentieth century, the Non-Aligned Movement developed out of the desire of some nations to side neither with the United States nor the Soviet Union. Today the movement continues to seek a third way between capitalism and communism.

Relations between Iran and some traditional rival countries have been improving. Saudi Arabia and Iran have softened relations toward each other. This warming is despite each country backing a different side in the Yemeni civil war, an ongoing conflict within the nation of Yemen in the southwest corner of the Arabian Peninsula, just below Saudi Arabia. The war is between the official government and a rebel group known as the Houthis. Each side claims to be the legitimate government. The war has killed at least 10,000 civilians and displaced millions more since it began in 2015. Some civilian deaths have been the direct result of targeted air strikes from the Saudi Air Force. The international organization Human Rights Watch said the Saudis were "killing civilians accurately." Due to lack of medicine and embargoes of humanitarian aid, outbreaks of diseases like cholera have also been responsible for civilian deaths.

International Relations

President Jimmy Carter cut diplomatic ties with Iran in 1979, and they have not been reestablished since. Switzerland handles all Iranian diplomacy for the United States. This is called being a *protecting power*.

Iran is a colorful and boisterous member of the international community. It has called the United States and some European nations spawn of Satan or Satan itself. It seeks to help countries that are trying to get out from under what they view as U.S. imperialism. Venezuela has been its major partner in this effort. The pair help other countries trying to disrupt U.S. influence in various regions. To this end, they have held summits aimed at using their influence in the oil markets to counter increased U.S. oil production through fracking. The two countries formed the Iran-Venezuela Bi-National Bank, which has sought to help grow industries throughout South

America. However, sanctions by the U.S. government have kept the bank from accomplishing much, though China has sought to help the bank operate in Latin America.

Iran has been accused of offering support to North Korea. North Korea is a rogue state that has achieved the development both of nuclear weapons and the means to deliver them. It is more of an outsider on the international stage than Iran. Its authoritarian communist government can be compared to Stalin's Soviet Union. Although Iran sees North Korea as a friend, it interacts carefully with the country.

Human Trafficking

Iran has been at the crossroads of Asia and Europe for thousands of years. The Silk Road of ancient times ran across Iran. Today that corridor is still used to transport goods. Sometimes these goods consist of human beings.

Iran is both an exporter and importer of human beings in slave-like conditions. The United Nations defines human trafficking as "the recruitment, transportation, transfer, harboring, or receipt of persons by improper means (such as force, abduction, fraud, or coercion) for an improper purpose including forced labor or sexual exploitation." Taking of human organs is also included in the definition.

A 2017 U.S. State Department report outlines the Iranian Army's use of human trafficking. Iran's Revolutionary Guard Corps was found to have forced foreign men—Afghanis who were living in a refugee camp inside Iran—to go fight in the Syrian War. Boys and young children from the camp were also sent to work in factories. The Guard sold women and older girls around the region for work in prostitution.

The United States reports that Iran fails to meet the minimum standards set for reducing trafficking. For social and economic reasons, Iran does not appear ready to alter its participation in human trafficking. Lack of outside access to Iran prevents a more detailed story from being told.

Illicit Drugs

Opium and its derivative drugs like heroin are illegal in Iran. However, law enforcement does not treat opiate users as harshly

Opium can be used in several ways. Sometimes, people smoke the opium with the assistance of a hookah.

as alcohol consumers. In the Muslim faith, alcohol is considered *haram*, or forbidden. Opiates are not as religiously objectionable. That doesn't mean that drug use is widely tolerated, though. Iran has a large government-sponsored system of opiate treatment centers. Addicts who are arrested for drug-related offenses can opt for free treatment. The alternative is very harsh. Drug possession of any kind in Iran is punishable by death.

That said, Iranian culture tolerates some drug use among older citizens. In the area known as the Golden Crescent, which runs across western Iran, Afghanistan, and part of Pakistan, opium smoking is common, especially given the drug's low price. The low price contributes to addiction, and many poor people become inadvertently addicted. Because opium eases pain and provides a feeling of well-being, the poor often use it as a substitute for effective medical treatment of disease.

Eighty percent of the world's opium is produced within the Golden Crescent. The nomadic tribes of this area have lived there for thousands of years. Opium is a part of their traditional medicine, but today, it is strictly reserved for the treatment of pain among the elderly, which is tolerated by the Iranian government.

Military

Iran is a country with a dramatic military history going back to the infancy of human civilization. The ancestors of Iran either created or were subjects of history's greatest empires. The Achaemenid Empire of the sixth century BCE, the Parthian Empire of the third century BCE, and the Sasanian Empire of the third century CE all emerged from what is today Iran. At various times, the area was under the control of Alexander the Great, the Ottoman Empire, and the Mongol Empire.

By the eighteenth century, during the decades preceding the American Revolution, Iran (then known as Persia) was one of the most powerful nations on Earth. It was a leader in the fields of art, science, culture, and trade throughout the region. Under the rule of Nader Shah, Iran grew in size and influence through military conquest. Although his military was outnumbered six to one, it took the capital of the Mughal Empire in three hours. Thus, Iran controlled most of what is today India. However, the power came at a price. Military expenditures hurt nonmilitary areas of the economy. Rebellions were common. Attempts to create compromises between

IN THE NEWS

An Island Dispute

A dispute over three islands in the Persian Gulf—Abu Musa, Greater Tunb, and Lesser Tunb—keeps Iran at odds with the United Arab Emirates (UAE). These island have been in dispute since the early 1970s when the British left after the independence of the UAE. The islands are important because of their position in strategic shipping lanes in the Persian Gulf. Since 1992, Iran has unilaterally built up a military presence on Abu Musa while restricting access to UAE police, teachers, and engineers. In spite of this conflict, the two countries cooperate when it is to each other's advantage.

Iranian soldiers patrolling the night streets of Shiraz.

Muslim sects failed and led to distrust between the groups. Nader Shah himself became fearful and inflicted brutal punishments for disloyalty, even on his own family. He was assassinated in 1747, and his empire quickly disintegrated.

After years of war with Russia, Iran's military was exhausted by the early twentieth century. The ruling family, the Qajar dynasty, had become weakened by rebellion. Their servants were assassinating family members. Eventually, they were ousted in a **coup**, and the new ruling family, the Pahlavis, would be the last royal family to rule Iran after 2,500 years of continuous monarchy.

The Pahlavi family took power in 1925. The first Pahlavi shah, Reza Shah, began rebuilding Iran's military. But that didn't last long. The Allied Powers of World War II invaded Iran to take oil fields in 1941. Both the Soviet and British military diverted oil and food to their own war efforts. Food was scarce for Iranians during the war, which fostered negative feelings about Europe, Russia, and, later, the United States. It was in this environment that the Iranian Revolution began. The future supreme leader Ayatollah Khomeini began his political career in activities opposed to European occupation.

The War and the Coup

The Allied invasion commenced in the late summer of 1941 and took less than a month to complete. Mohammad Reza Shah replaced his father as shah in September of that year. For the duration of World War II, the Soviets controlled oil fields in the north of Iran and the British controlled oil fields in the south. The United States brokered a deal during the Tehran summit between U.S. President Franklin D. Roosevelt, British Prime Minister Winston Churchill, and Soviet Premier Joseph Stalin that guaranteed Iran would return to being an independent nation after the war.

After the United States pressured the Soviet Union and Great Britain to leave Iran after World War II, the shah rebuilt a primarily defensive military. But he did harbor ambitions that one day Iran would return to its position as the dominant regional nation. He also wanted Iran to wield international influence.

Most monarchs have a prime minister. The shah was no different. His prime minister, democratically elected in 1953, was Mohammad Mosaddegh. Prime ministers vary in their power. For example, in the United Kingdom, the prime minister is on a similar executive level with the president of the United States.

In 1953, the power of the Iranian prime minister was growing. Mosaddegh was popular. He was progressive. He felt that Iranians should have more control over their own destinies. For obvious reasons, he clashed with the autocratic shah.

August 1953 saw the Iranian parliament debate and successfully pass a law nationalizing Iranian oil fields. This upset the United States and the United Kingdom. The British had built the world's largest oil refinery in Iran during World War II. Also, the United States had invested heavily in developing the Iranian oil industry. (The Soviet Union left Iran after the war in an agreement that had the United States withdraw its postwar troops from China.)

British and American spy agencies helped the shah force Prime Minister Mosaddegh from office in late August 1953. In spite of what typically happens in a coup, Mosaddegh was not killed. He lived the rest of his life under house arrest. Upon his death in 1967, the shah's government denied him a funeral.

In contrast, near the end of the shah's rule, he held a 2,500-year anniversary party for the Iranian monarchy. The party was lavish,

Although he was ultimately forced from office, there were people who supported Prime Minister Mosaddegh. A pro-Mosaddegh rally in the streets of Tehran is pictured here.

yet the shah was so unpopular by that time that he and his family were the only Iranians in attendance. The party was largely attended by international business and political allies.

Terrorist Groups

A 1996 resolution of the UN General Assembly defines terrorism as "criminal acts intended or calculated to provoke a state of terror in the general public, a group of persons or particular persons for political purposes" and states that these acts "are in any circumstance unjustifiable, whatever the considerations of a political, philosophical, ideological, racial, ethnic, religious or any other nature that may be invoked to justify them." For example, a government battle against an armed militant group would not be considered an act of terrorism for either party. A government killing the unarmed family members of a militant group would be considered an act of terrorism on the part of the government.

Terrorism in Iran is both a policy function of the government and a tactic of its opposition. From its outset, the Iranian government has seen terrorism as a justified tool for the progress of its Islamic Revolution. The birth of the Islamic Republic of Iran was witnessed by 52 Americans held hostage in the U.S. embassy for more than a year. The hostages were taken by students in response to the United States letting the ousted shah into the United States for cancer treatment. The ordeal went on for 444 days before the Americans were released.

To this end, the Iranian government uses terroristic tactics like bombings, assassinations, and kidnappings against its enemies at home and abroad. Iranian groups opposed to the government often face mass arrest, street punishment, or the killing of family members. The People's Mojahedin Organization of Iran, a former militant Iranian resistance group that renounced violence in the 2000s, is one of the largest groups opposed to the Islamic Revolution. It continues to be a target of Iranian authorities.

The 52 American hostages were released after 444 days. Here they are at a hospital after their release.

Iran supports terrorism around the world. However, its support focuses on groups that in one way or another aim at expanding the religious and political ideology of the Islamic Revolution. Most of the groups supported by Iran, like Hezbollah, are dedicated to fighting against Israel and establishing a Shi'ite theocracy for the whole of the Middle East.

In recent years, Iran has kicked up its support for Muslim terrorist organizations operating out of Africa. The United States has labeled Iran the world's top state sponsor of terror. This means that of all the governments on the planet, Iran sends more money, guns, and soldiers to terrorist groups than any other. Iran faces security challenges based primarily on its outlier status as a theocratic, terrorism-exporting nation.

Text-Dependent Questions

1. How long was Iran under continual rule by a monarch prior to the Islamic Revolution?

2. How did Iran create a stalemate on the battlefield with Iraq in the Iran-Iraq War?

3. Explain the purpose of the alliance between Iran and Venezuela.

Research Project

The Islamic Revolution did not start out as a religious movement. Opposition to the autocratic shah of Iran began as a movement of aligned political parties across democratic, socialist, and religious ideologies. As religious influence grew after 1979, all nonreligious parties were eventually outlawed. Create a time line of the revolution, noting when each of the nonreligious parties become illegal and what became of their leaders.

CHAPTER 2

Government and Politics

Iran's government was born out of the Islamic Revolution of 1979. Prior to the revolution, the government operated as a hereditary monarchy in which power was concentrated in an autocratic leader called the shah. Though the shah of Iran was a monarchical title that went back 2,500 years, the pre-1979 government was structured by the Allies after World War II. They attempted to give Iran the workings of a constitutional monarchy similar to European governments. However, that was far from how politics and power actually worked in Iran. The shah was the ruler and exercised frequent repression of any opposition.

Similarly, that is how Iran's post-1979 government works. Outwardly, the government is organized along the lines of that of the United States with three branches of government, with one

Words to Understand

Judiciary: A network of courts within a society and their relationship to each other.

Majlis: The common name for the lower house of the Iranian legislature, roughly equivalent to the U.S. House of Representatives.

Referendum: A decision on a particular issue put up to a popular vote.

Zoroastrian: A follower of Zoroastrianism, an ancient monotheistic religion native to Iran.

Posters of supreme leaders, current and past, can be found throughout the city streets of Iran. They even appear on the entrances of some mosques.

Iran's Government and Legal System at a Glance

Independence	April 1, 1979 (Islamic Republic of Iran proclaimed)
National Holiday	Republic Day, April 1
National Symbol(s)	Lion
Constitution	Previous 1906; latest adopted October 24, 1979, effective December 3, 1979
Legal System	Religious legal system based on secular and Islamic law
Voting Eligibility	18 years or older; universal

important exception: Iran's ultimate authority in law and military matters sits with the supreme leader.

Not only does the supreme leader have the final say in governmental matters, he is the country's religious leader as well. This makes Iran a modern theocratic state. Iran's constitution states that the country's government has a "fundamental role in ensuring the uninterrupted process of the revolution of Islam." The principle from which the supreme leaders derives his power comes from the Shi'a form of Islam and is called the Guardianship of the Islamic Jurist. Belief in the absolute form of this principle leaves no room for separation of church and state, such as in the United States. Islamic governments are to be headed by a *faqeeh*, or guardian jurist, who is to have final say over both religious and political matters. In Iran, this extends to elections and freedom of the press as well.

Government Type

Iran's government has been described as having a mix of theocratic and democratic elements. Under the powerful office of the supreme leader of Iran are three branches of government: legislative, executive, and judicial. This structure of the government is similar to that of the United States. However, in Iran the supreme leader has the right to intrude on any of these parts of government. He has final say over all political and military matters.

Moreover, like the United States, Iran has a legislature with two branches. Even so, those branches are not equal, as they are in the United States. One branch, the Consultative Assembly, makes the laws, whereas the other, the Guardian Council, reviews and approves the laws.

Constitution

The Iranian constitution spells out both the religious and civil responsibilities of government. Article 1 of the constitution establishes Iran as an Islamic Republic. Article 2 sets forth a belief in one God—as in "There is no god but Allah"—which is the basic creed of Islam. It also sets out that the government of Iran makes its laws based on divine revelation.

In addition to spelling out the religious authority of government, the document sets forth many civil responsibilities. The

The current supreme leader of Iran is Ali Khamenei.

government is responsible for, among other things, free education and physical training, the elimination of "undesirable" discrimination, and planning a just economic system.

Although Iran does not consider itself to be a socialist government, many sectors of the economy, including media, telecommunications, banking, and mining, are specifically spelled out in the constitution as being owned by the government. The constitution lists these and other economic sectors as "mother industries."

The current constitution of Iran was adopted by a public vote on December 2 and 3, 1979. This constitution replaced the previous constitution of 1906. The current constitution was amended in 1989 to change some of the qualifications necessary to be the supreme leader and to create the Expediency Discernment Council, along with other minor modifications. The purpose of the council is to settle disputes in the legislature when important laws prove difficult to pass. Members are appointed by the supreme leader to five-year terms.

Revisions to the constitution require the approval of the supreme leader. If he is willing to allow proposed changes, then he issues an edict to that effect. This begins the process of changing the constitution. Next, a Council for Revision of the Constitution is formed to write new amendments. Once amendments are written and agreed to by the council, they are put to a popular vote.

The council consists of government officials advised by three university professors. At times, the officials and the advisors have clashed. Ahmad Azari Qomi was a conservative religious scholar who advised the council throughout the 1980s and 1990s. Today, he is remembered as a dissident. He has the distinction of having been arrested for political crimes by both the shah and the supreme leader. Though a conservative, he criticized the supreme leader in 1997 for direct intimidation of liberal professors through state security forces. This led to his arrest, and the ayatollah went on national television accusing Qomi of treason. Qomi was eventually released and died of natural causes in 1999.

Some aspects of the constitution are unalterable. The Islamic character of the government, Islam as the official religion, the democratic aspect of government, and the right to governmental changes through **referendum** are among those aspects that cannot be altered.

Iranian National Holiday

The Iranian national holiday is called Iranian Islamic Republic Day. It is celebrated as a public holiday on or around April 1st. Due to differences in western and Islamic calendars, it sometimes falls on March 31st or April 2nd. The day recognizes the formal proclamation of the end of the shah's rule and the establishment of the Islamic Republic of Iran by popular referendum in 1979. This was a different referendum than the one that approved the constitution in December of that year.

IN THE NEWS

Islamic Seminary Burned by Protesters

A religious teaching school in northwest Iran was attacked by protesters in the summer of 2018, who burned the structure to the ground. This was unusual for protests in Iran. Attacking the Islamic nature of the Iranian government is illegal, and protesters usually avoid it in their message. Even in the most violent protests, protesters have attacked government buildings but not religious ones; to burn a religious building to the ground was unprecedented. The attack on the school and the "Down with Dictators" slogans represent a change in protest tactics that includes attacking the religious nature of the Iranian government.

The Legal System

The Iranian civil **judiciary** consists of three types of courts: the general courts, special courts, and administrative courts.

The general courts in Iran have authority over criminal, civil, family, and juvenile matters. Preliminary and appellate courts fall in this category, including the Supreme Court. Like the United States, the Supreme Court of Iran has the final say in legal matters. The court is also responsible for hearing any offenses concerning the president. The entire judiciary is run by the chief justice (sometimes referred to as the head of judiciary), who is appointed by the supreme leader.

Iranians take to the streets each year to celebrate Iranian Islamic Republic Day.

Since 1979, there have been five chief justices. The current chief justice is Sadeq Larijani (*left*).

Special courts include revolutionary courts, which were set up after the Islamic Revolution. Their purpose is to hear cases related to national security, which can mean a lot of things in Iran. Revolutionary courts have heard cases related to drug smuggling and political dissent that in their view undermines the Islamic Republic. Military and clergy courts are also a part of the specialized courts.

The administrative courts handle disputes between people and governmental and other public institutions and interpretations of regulations. Preliminary administrative courts are usually attached to a particular government branch, like the Tax Commission and Municipality Commission.

Members of the court achieve their status by being recognized as leading legal scholars, though the process for deciding who is a legal scholar is obscure. Generally, a body of legal and religious scholars, along with sitting judges, determine who should be recognized as a scholar qualified to sit on the Supreme Court.

Political Parties

Iran has many political parties, though most fall inside one of two groups: the Principlists and the Reformists. Several dissident parties are also active inside and outside of the country. The dissident parties span the entire traditional political spectrum from nationalist to socialist. There are even active monarchists seeking a return of the shah. However, membership in these parties is small, and the government severely oppresses members if they reside inside Iran.

Parties are free to espouse economic policies that run the gamut from capitalist to socialist. However, no party can run afoul of the basic tenets of Iran's Islamic constitution, such as the supremacy of Islamic law or the supremacy of the supreme leader. Parties that drift in those directions are outlawed because they want to abolish the Islamic aspects of the Iranian government.

Political party membership in Iran tends to focus on profession first and political beliefs second. There are Principlist parties for the clergy, engineers, teachers, physicians, and other professionals. The same is true of Reformist parties.

Head of the Reformists, Mohammed Reza Aref, waves to his supporters during a campaign in Tehran.

The Principlist camp supports the current structure of the Iranian government and its aim of seeking to expand the Islamic Revolution around the world. They are often referred to in the American press as "hard-liners." The Reformists still support the basic foundations of the Islamic Revolution but want to see Iran seek diplomatic solutions to strained relations with the Western democracies. In exchange, they are willing to forego the militaristic and terroristic methods of expanding the Islamic Revolution.

The major parties of the Principlist camp include the following:

- *Combatant Clergy Association.* This is what is referred to as an "elite party" in Iranian politics. The party consists of Islamic clergy members at the highest levels. They don't field candidates themselves but support candidates of other parties. In addition, they have a lot of behind-the-scenes influence among members of the Iranian Revolutionary Guard and the Guardian Council.

- *Society of Seminary Teachers of Qom.* This is another "elite party" made up of religious scholars whose main job is to decide who gets to move up the ranks of the Islamic clergy in Iran. Members are chosen by the supreme leader. They exert political influence over who gets permission to run for office from the supreme leader.

- *Islamic Coalition Party.* This is a traditionalist party. A traditionalist party is one that supports the religious aims of expanding the Islamic Revolution to other countries. The party has been active since just after the Islamic Revolution in Iran. It is allied with the Combatant Clergy Association. Members are primarily merchants, shopkeepers, and other middle-class businessmen. The fact that membership is made up of older people gives the party a stodgy image. Younger people tend to join other Principlist parties.

- *Society of Devotees of the Islamic Revolution.* This party was formed shortly after the Iran-Iraq War. It consists primarily of veterans and their widows. The party was formed as a protection force for Islamic Revolution monuments, but in reality, this is the party that brutally attacks anti-government protesters in

A meeting of the Seminary Teachers of Qom.

the streets and even in their homes. In like manner, they also perform "extra-judicial" arrests, meaning they take people and put them in prison without formal arrest or trial. Former president Mahmoud Ahmadinejad was a founding member.

- *Front of Islamic Revolution Stability.* The most far-right in Iran, this party stands against what members call "sedition," which to them is any kind of anti-revolutionary expression, and "deviant current," which is the influence of Western nations on Iranian society.

- *YEKTA Front.* This party was founded by supporters of former Iranian president Mahmoud Ahmadinejad. Members support Ahmadinejad's positions on economic development and the role of the clergy in government. Ahmadinejad sought to diminish the power of the clergy while supporting a centralized approach to economic development.

Prominent Reformist parties include the following:

- *Association of Combatant Clerics.* This Reformist party, which has existed since the mid-1980s, consists of clerics who want to limit clerical influence in civil matters, though not to the extent of completely getting rid of clerical power.

- **Islamic Labour Party.** This center-left Reformist party concentrates on economic development and worker rights. It is not socialist but advocates for a free marketplace and government programs that incentivize projects that require a lot of workers.

- **Executives of Construction Party.** This party is allied with businessmen and developers and partners with the Islamic Labour Party on matters that benefit both. It is a free-market party with an emphasis on government policies that promote large development projects.

- **National Trust Party.** This Reformist party takes a populist approach with calls for more freedoms, restrictions on the power of the supreme leader, and better relations with the United States. The party manages to keep itself running afoul of anti-Islamic law by saying that it is for an Islamic state, just one that doesn't have a powerful religious leader deciding nonreligious government policy.

- **Nedaye Iranian (NEDA) Party.** Probably Iran's most left-wing legal party, NEDA is a Reformist party that advocates for socialist policies but still supports the theocratic state.

- **Moderation and Development Party.** This Reformist party consists of traditional centrists who support economic development over the social development of the Islamic Revolution. It often allies itselves with the Islamic Labour Party and the Executives of Construction party.

In both Principlist and Reformist camps, various professional associations double as political parties of a sort. These associations produce lists of candidates that they support, similar to the kind of campaign literature made by unions in the United States. Outside of their reach within a profession, however, they exert little influence. In the Principlist camp, these include the Islamic Society of Engineers, the Islamic Association of Physicians, the Islamic Society of Employees, and the Islamic Society of Athletes. The Assembly of Qom Seminary Scholars and Researchers, the Islamic Association of Teachers, the Islamic Association of Engineers, and the Islamic Association of University Instructors are active professional political associations on the Reformist side.

Because they have been oppressed at home, a number of banned Iranian parties have established a presence in Europe and the United States. Stationing themselves in Western democracies enables them to raise money, which has helped facilitate awareness of issues that the Iranian government would rather the world did not know about. Executions of Iranians for minor crimes and evidence of government corruption are two issues that have been brought to light because of these organizations.

The Executive Branch

The executive branch is on an equal level with the legislature. It is led by a president who is elected by direct vote to a four-year term. A president may serve two terms or a total of eight years, as with the office of the presidency in the United States. However, in the United States, the president is elected indirectly through the Electoral College. In Iran, candidates are first approved by the supreme leader and then elected by popular vote. The presidential candidate with the most votes wins. The president is known as the head of government, whereas the supreme leader is the head of state. This is a similar arrangement to the United Kingdom's prime minister and monarch.

The office of the presidency in Iran has considerably less power than in other countries. The president cannot veto legislation, enter into treaties, set regional policy, or even appoint some members of

Similar to the United States, the Iranian president has a cabinet, too. Pictured here, the president holds a cabinet meeting.

his cabinet. These powers are reserved for the supreme leader, who appoints military, security, and even science ministers. Ambassadors to other Arab countries are appointed by the Qods Force, which is the country's elite military force that answers directly to the supreme leader. If the United States had a similar arrangement, it would be something like the head of the Navy SEALs having the authority to appoint ambassadors to Mexico, Canada, and the Caribbean nations.

The Legislative Branch

Iran's legislative body is also known as the Iranian parliament. The Consultative Assembly functions as the lower house of parliament. This body is commonly referred to as the **Majlis**. The currently 290 members of the assembly were last elected in 2016.

Elections in Iran are only somewhat free. Candidates can be disqualified by the Guardian Council, which functions as an upper house of parliament. Right from the start, Iranians are limited to candidates approved by the government. Also, transparency varies with each election. The Guardian Council also has the authority to limit the amount of election data released to the public.

The president speaks at the Iranian parliament.

Anti-American sentiment in the Iranian parliament.

Accusations of Tampering

In 2009, Iranian presidential elections incited nationwide protests after then-president Mahmoud Ahmadinejad was declared the winner only three hours after polls closed. Protesters accused the government of tampering with the results. Irregularities included the government refusing to release the results of individual polling stations or give that information to candidates. The United States, Europe, and most other recognized democracies have laws requiring the publishing of polling station results.

Of the 290 members in the Majlis, 285 are directly elected, with five members reserved for minority religious and cultural groups such as Jews, Christians, **Zoroastrians**, and Armenians. These groups decide among themselves how to choose their delegates.

The Guardian Council operates as a review body for the Consultative Assembly. The council is made up of 12 Islamic scholars. Members are appointed by the Head of the Judiciary. So although the Guardian Council is part of the legislature, it also has a foot in the judicial branch. The body has complete veto power. Each piece of legislation must be voted on twice: once on whether the proposed law is compatible with Islam, and then again on whether it is compatible with the Iranian constitution. All 12 members vote on a bill's constitutional compatibility. Only six vote on whether a bill is compatible with Islam. If a bill is rejected, it is sent back to the Consultative Assembly for corrections.

If the legislature cannot agree on a bill, it then goes to yet another body. This one is called the Expediency Discernment Council. All members are appointed by the supreme leader. In this sense, this body also has a foot in the executive branch. The council is part of the highest echelon of Iranian government, a feature of the office of the Supreme Leadership Authority.

The Judicial Branch

Like other branches of government, the judicial branch falls under the authority of the supreme leader. The highest authority on the court is the chief justice. The supreme leader appoints the chief justice who heads the supreme court of Iran. Chiefs serve for a term of five years. The Iranian Supreme Court works differently than the American style of Supreme Court that is found in judiciaries around the world. Instead of having a single body make the final decision about cases, the Iranian Supreme Court is divided into criminal and civil branches. The branches hear lower court cases and either annul or affirm their decisions.

Below the Supreme Court sit all the other courts. All of these courts are responsible for following the Iranian legal code. Harsh punishments like flogging and stoning can be meted out by these courts. The Iranian legal code is based on Sharia law, and the brutal punishments in the code come from criminal punishments published in the Qu'ran, which is 1,500 years old.

All judges are supervised by the High Council of the Judiciary. The High Council consists of the chief justice of the Supreme Court, the attorney general, and three religious jurists. The High Council is responsible for the structure and rules of the court and recommending judges. Court rules cover everything from courthouse hours to submission of evidence.

Rights of the accused in Iran include a presumption of innocence, but the burden of proof (beyond a reasonable doubt in American courts) is not spelled out in the constitution and can vary from court to court. Individuals in Iran cannot be prosecuted for acts that weren't crimes when they were committed. Although the legal code spells out a right to *habeas corpus*, the right to be free from arrest without specific charges, no mechanism exists forcing the police to inform the arrestee of their charges, and the right is often violated.

The Courthouse of Tehran was built between 1938 and 1946. This building is where the High Council meets today.

The right to representation is spelled out in the Iranian constitution. A person charged with a crime can chose any lawyer he or she likes. Be that as it may, judges have the power to prevent lawyers from being present during interrogations.

The Office of the Supreme Leader

The supreme leader is the final political, military, and religious authority in Iran. He can veto laws and dismiss any member of the president's cabinet, not just the ones he appoints himself. His say is required for use of military force, and his office is directly responsible for all important foreign matters. The supreme leader also gets to decide on the transparency of elections. Each election in Iran has had different levels of transparency as set forth by the supreme leader.

A ministry of foreign affairs is the government agency that carries out a government's international policies. However, in the case of Iran, the ministry has been relegated to ceremonial functions, with real power in foreign affairs held by the Supreme National Security Council. The exception came in 2013 when the council delegated responsibility for negotiating the nuclear deal to the ministry.

Technically, a body called the Assembly of Experts is responsible for electing the supreme leader and has the authority to dismiss him. However, candidates for the Assembly of Experts

must be approved by the supreme leader before they are put up for a public vote. There are currently 88 members of the Assembly of Experts who are elected to eight-year terms.

Parliament Summons President for the First Time

U.S. sanctions over nuclear weapons development went back into force in the summer of 2018. By early August, the Iranian economy was suffering uncertainty, and its currency was sinking in value. In an unprecedented move, the Islamic Consultative Assembly called the president to stand in front of the legislative body and answer questions about how he would handle an already fragile economy in light of renewed sanctions.

Text-Dependent Questions

1. Name the two political camps in Iranian politics.

2. True or false: The supreme leader may appoint presidential cabinet ministers.

3. How many terms can an Iranian president serve?

Research Projects

1. Imagine the Iranian Consultative Assembly has proposed a law. Make a flowchart showing the different deliberative bodies that bill would go through before becoming law.

2. Research a current Iranian head of state, such as the president, chief justice, or speaker of the parliament. Write a brief biography of this figure, including personal background, legislative, legal, or religious philosophies, achievements and controversies, and other information.

CHAPTER 3
Economy

A look at a country's economy can better tell about the happiness of its people and efficiency of its society than can government statements or forward-thinking plans. Iran has accomplished several goals that it set out on 40 years ago. The country established an Islamic-style banking system, shunning Western banks. Sanctions have made a separate banking system a necessity because many international banks are barred from doing business with Iran.

Advances for women have been slow in Iran. Only recently have women been allowed to sit as judges, but only for minor cases like traffic tickets. Women also make up only a fraction of college professors, and there, too, they teach rudimentary classes and are shunned from research.

Although the country has a robust educational system and everyone has access to an education, many working-class young

Words to Understand

Arable: Used to describe land capable of being used for farming.

Hijab: A headscarf worn by some Muslim women.

Inflation: An increase in prices of goods and services over time.

Murabaha: A system of financing compatible with Sharia law in which the buyer agrees to pay a determined profit margin plus the cost of an item instead of paying interest on a purchase.

Usury: The process of lending money at unreasonably high interest rates.

This nineteenth-century building houses the first public bank of Iran—the Tejarat Bank.

Iran's Economy at a Glance

Currency	Rial; 2017 exchange rate: 32,769.7 rials per U.S. dollar
Labor Force	30.5 million; 16.3 percent in agriculture, 35.1 percent in industry, 48.6 percent in services
Per Capita Income (PPP)	$21,000 (2017)
Inflation Rate	9.9 percent (2017 estimate)
Gross Domestic Product (GDP)	$1.645 trillion (2017)
Overall Unemployment	12.4 percent (2017)
Industries	Services; manufacturing; agriculture
Imports	Industrial supplies, capital goods, foodstuffs and other consumer goods, technical services
Import Partners	United Arab Emirates 29.8 percent, China 12.7 percent, Turkey 4.4 percent, South Korea 4 percent, Germany 4 percent
Exports	Petroleum, chemical and petrochemical products, fruits and nuts, carpets, cement, ore
Export Partners	China 27.5 percent, India 15.1 percent, South Korea 11.4 percent, Turkey 11.1 percent, Italy 5.7 percent, Japan 5.3 percent

people still leave high school before graduation because of family financial pressure.

Agriculture has been the country's most troubling sector. Despite efforts to improve farming on what is more than enough **arable** land to feed the country, Iran must import food from other countries just to feed its population. Inefficiencies of traditional farming practices have slowed efforts to modernize Iran's farms.

Currency and Banking System

The Iranian currency is the rial, which dates back to 1798 when the country was a monarchy ruled by a shah. Until 2012, Iranian oil exchanges traded in U.S. dollars, but frustration with U.S. handling of Iran's nuclear ambitions led the country to switch from dollars to euros. The rial had been trading at a rate of between 30 and 130 rials to the U.S. dollar in the decades between oil discovery in the 1930s and the overthrow of the shah in 1979. The value of the rial slid immediately after the Islamic Revolution. The reason for the slide was because foreign companies and governments took their

Rial banknotes feature images of the supreme leader.

money out of the country, a situation called "capital flight." The new Iranian government had not yet been formed, and no one knew how the country would operate until the new constitution was voted on. Would foreign businesses be nationalized? Would foreign money be seized? Many wealthy businesses and companies in the country felt it was best to get their capital out.

The rial has stayed at a fractional value ever since. For example, 50,000 rials were equal to around $1.19 as of late 2018. That value was particularly low due to the reinstatement of sanctions by the United States over Iran's nuclear program. The monetary symbol of the rial looks like this: ریال

Iran's banking system is a government-run industry based on Sharia law and tradition. Mainly, this means that the charging of interest, in the Western sense, is considered **usury** and is forbidden within Iran. Iran does conduct international business and has "zones" where interest banking can take place, but ordinary Iranians are tied to an Islamic banking system. In this system, profits are made primarily on fees. This includes some of the same kinds of fees seen in American banking, such as those for checking accounts.

Other kinds of fees would seem strange to American consumers. For example, instead of charging interest as a percentage of a loan, banks make their money by charging an upfront fee. If someone wants to borrow the equivalent of $10,000, they would pay something like a $2,000 fee upfront, receive the $10,000, and pay the principal back over time. This is called *murabaha*.

Labor Force

Iran's labor force is measured as those age 10 or over who are part of the economically active population. Though the minimum legal working age is 15, exemptions exist in a number of sectors. Family businesses and what are called "domestic workshops" can utilize workers younger than 15. Domestic workshops include those that specialize in small-scale manufacturing, like jewelers, as long as the work is done out of a home.

Iran has a modern labor force in that working Iranians are active in both the low-skilled and high-skilled sectors. Iran has more than 30 million workers, and the economy is ranked 21st worldwide in the size of its labor force. In 2017, the industrial sector, which includes manufacturing, construction, petroleum, and mining, took up 36 percent of the Iranian economy. Agriculture contributed to just 10 percent of the economy. The largest sector was service at 48 percent, which includes government workers.

Women make up just 15 percent the workforce. Only six other countries have a lower female participation rate. Due to reforms in the early 2000s, women can serve in professional positions previously denied to them, such as employment as lower-level judges and professors.

Younger workers have fared poorly. The unemployment rate is higher than 29 percent for those under 24. The average age of Iranian workers is getting older every year, and younger workers are denied access to education and opportunities that would expose them to the latest ideas in the science and business sectors. But education alone is not a determining factor in who is more likely to be unemployed. Since the 1979 revolution, the number of college graduates in Iran has shot up 25 percent. However, many young and educated Iranians are unemployed. They cannot put

If working for the family, children under 15 can and will work. Pictured here, a young boy assists with the herding of his family's sheep.

A group of women work together in a workshop to create beautiful rugs.

their educations to use because of economic stagnation due to international nuclear sanctions and the mismanagement of expansion schemes by the government. On the positive side, adult literacy has exceeded 85 percent since the revolution due to a government-sponsored education effort.

Ideology, religious or otherwise, does not seem to be the motivation of today's Iranian protester. Instead, economic troubles are the focus for Iranians taking to the streets and appealing to their government. The *Los Angeles Times* quoted one protester whose own thoughts echoed the feelings of many young and educated Iranians. He said, "I don't care about politics or domestic or foreign policy or the nuclear deal. I just need a predictable future."

Poverty

Poverty in Iran is hard to pin down. Official estimates put 8.1 percent of the population of Iran in poverty. In spite of that, many reformers in parliament say poverty is actually much higher. While arguing for the ouster of the labor minister, a member of the assembly said in March 2018 that the poverty level was really more like 80 percent.

Protests in large cities, such as Tehran, have become more frequent in Iran. Many are protesting the government and economy.

IN THE NEWS

Female Activist Suffers for Taking Off Hijab

During anti-government street protests in early 2018, several women got social media attention by taking off their **hijabs** in public and waving them from poles. The hijab, a scarf that goes over the head, is required religious attire for women in Iranian public spaces. Many women were arrested for this rebellious act, and some were not heard from for weeks. One female activist who dared to wave her hijab a second time after arrest got a 20-year prison sentence. Another woman, Masih Alinejad, fled Iran after police targeted her for waving her hijab from a pole. In London, she learned government media in Iran was circulating a fake news report that she had been raped. She was unable to reach her family to discredit the story.

Learn about a cause of poverty in Iran.

Poverty is one of the reasons for a series of street protests that began in Iran in January of 2018. The protests have only accelerated since the renewal of U.S. sanctions against Iran in August of 2018.

Part of the problem in determining the true poverty level is something called **inflation**. For various economic reasons, prices of goods and services have been steadily rising for years, in both Iran and other countries. U.S. sanctions play a part in this. The official poverty level in Iran is 7 million rials a day, which is about $5.15. Because of inflation over the span of 2017 and 2018, the real figure is more than three times that, about 25 million rials a day.

Enduring poverty seems something the Iranian government is willing to tolerate in its effort to either build, or not build, a nuclear weapon. Iran has no stated goal of building a weapon, though some members of the international community suspect otherwise.

Enduring a Drought

The Iranian government did not say or do much about a devastating 2018 drought crisis that was the worst since the last century. It has contributed to the loss of 10 percent of Iran's farmable land. Lakes have turned to desert in some places. Part of the reason is seasonal drought, part of it could be global warming, and part of it is from mismanagement. The relationship between the farmers and government officials deteriorated throughout 2018, with several farmers injured in protests.

A homeless man begs for alms.

Agriculture

Iran has a large area of land—more than a third of the country—suitable for farming. In fact, the total acreage of potential agricultural land in Iran is greater than that of all of Europe. However, much of the suitable lands remains unfarmed due to political, economic, and educational reasons. First, government policies make investment in farming risky. After the revolution, many farmers claimed the land they worked as their own. These farmers were tenants who did not own the land. The government has been slow to solve the disputes satisfactorily, so farm investment remains low. Second, the land tends to be farmed using antiquated techniques, which has ended up putting many farms out of business. Crop yields are low, and Iran has to import food to feed its population.

The effort to modernize Iranian farming began with plans to innovate new agricultural machinery and technologies. The result has been impressively successful: Today Iran is a net exporter of heavy tractors used in farming. But making and having good machines does not mean that farmers entrenched in centuries-old practices are going to adopt them. Farming tends to be done by several isolated

Although land is plentiful, Iran still under-utilizes it for agricultural purposes.

cultures within Iran. Their hesitance to adopt new technology is part of what keeps these communities in poverty and requires Iran to import a good portion of its food.

That said, the largest crops Iran produces are wheat, rice, barley, sugar, pistachios, saffron, and tea. Wheat is Iran's only essential surplus crop. The country is the world's 12th-largest exporter of wheat and leads all nations in exports of pistachios and saffron, the world's most expensive spice. (By weight, it is more expensive than gold.) However, pistachios and saffron are not considered essential, and Iran's leadership in these areas makes only a dent in the overall food-trade shortage.

Energy

Iran has become energy self-sufficient and is considered an energy superpower. Not only does Iran have multiple oil reserves and export its oil around the world, it also builds and maintains its own power plants, including hydroelectric, oil, and natural gas–fueled facilities. The government has ambitious plans for nuclear energy, but so far only one plant has been built. It was completed with the help of Russia, and its output has not been efficient. The power it has generated costs six times that of power generated by U.S. nuclear plants.

A man rides a tractor on his farm. Technology like this has helped Iranian farmers flourish.

In addition to oil, Iran also has hydroelectric (top) and thermal (bottom) power sources.

An oil rig off the coast of Kish Island.

Text-Dependent Questions

1. What form of law sets forth the rules and regulations of banking in Iran?

2. What is the minimum legal working age in Iran?

3. Explain the problems faced by the Iranian agricultural industry.

Research Project

Compare farming in the United States and Iran, including overall crop yields, farming methods, and the amounts of unused land. Make a chart comparing different aspects of farming in each country, including technologies used, crops grown, and other information.

Quality of Life

ranians who supported the revolution in 1979 were not primarily interested in religious matters. They wanted a better life. They experienced corruption when seeking recourse from government agencies, a lack of opportunity in their working lives, and an inadequate social safety net. The promise of the revolution gave Iranians hope. When it came to power, the new government planned large-scale building projects that would produce jobs and stimulate the economy. It passed laws to improve social programs. The results have been improvements in some areas of economic and social life, whereas other areas have experienced failures and a slide into the same kind of problems and corruption as under the shah.

Words to Understand

Desalination: The process through which salt is removed from ocean water so that the water is drinkable.

Malnutrition: A medical condition caused by a lack of food, or a diet deficient in certain nutrients.

Mortality rate: The number of deaths for a given population over a fixed amount of time.

Productivity: In economics, the measurement of economic gain from human or other efforts.

Even though Iranians annually celebrate their 1979 revolution, there is still much to be attained.

Iran's Quality of Life at a Glance

Life Expectancy at Birth	74 years
Maternal Mortality Rate	25 deaths/100,000 live births
Infant Mortality Rate	15.9 deaths/1,000 live births
Physician Density	1.49/1,000 population
Prevalence of HIV/AIDS in Adults	0.1 percent
Prevalence of Obesity in Adults	25.8 percent
Improved Sanitation Facility Access	Urban: 92.8 percent of population; rural: 82.3 percent of population; total: 90 percent of population
Improved Drinking Water Source	Urban: 97.7 percent of population; rural: 92.1 percent of population; total: 96.2 percent of population
Literacy	86.8 percent of population
Electricity Access	98.6 percent of population
Telecommunications Access	Fixed line: 37 subscriptions per 100 people; cellular: 98 subscriptions per 100 people
Internet Use	44.1 percent of population
Broadcast Media	State-run with 13 national channels, approximately 34 provincial channels, and several international channels

Basic Human Needs

Iran has made great strides in providing health care, clean water access, and sanitation to its citizens since the postrevolutionary transition. However, work still needs to be done to ensure greater economic equality, especially in urban areas where housing prices can be high.

Nutrition and Basic Medical Care

The 1990s were a time of transition for Iran. Almost 20 percent of Iranian children were malnourished. The government did not keep **malnutrition** statistics on individuals over the age of 16. Body mass index statistics (based on the relationship between a person's height and weight) kept on adolescents and adults at the time showed that growth in height lagged behind weight increases. Slower growth rates indicate that malnourishment was leading to lower average heights of those over 12 years old at the time of the study.

Today, much has changed in terms of access to food. However, the quality of available food still presents a problem. A large migration of people away from farms and into cities in the early 2000s

A man sorts through the snack items at an Iranian market.

Some Iranian Contributions to Nutrition (and Other Fun Stuff)

Iranian cuisine has given the world several good foods. The peach comes from Persia. The Romans called them *persica*. Spinach would not plague dinner plates if it weren't for ancient Persia. The Chinese called it the "herb of Persia." The Dutch would never have had their mid-Renaissance tulip craze had it not been for Iran cultivating the first tulips. But most important, though not exactly related to nutrition: Cookies and ice cream come from Persia. Does that mean cookie-dough ice cream is a remix?

decreased overall food production. Imports of processed foods have reduced hunger but have left poorer Iranians with a junk-food diet. This has produced obesity problems not unlike what the United States is experiencing.

Health care in Iran is provided by a combination of governmental, private, and charitable organizations. Those who cannot afford private-sector insurance can get care through a network of private clinics that receive government and charitable funding. Because of improvements in prenatal care after a government revamp of the country's primary care network, child and maternal **mortality rates** have fallen. Bloomberg News ranked Iran's system as the 30th most efficient in the world in a 2016 survey, ahead of the United States and Brazil.

The high quality of Iran's health-care system attracts medical tourists. These are people who travel outside of their own country to get medical care, usually because it is better than what they might receive in their home country. Iran attracts people in need of care from Iraq, Syria, Pakistan, and other countries. Lack of access to care because of war is one of the motivating factors of medical tourists to Iran.

Water and Sanitation

During the mid-1990s, only 20 percent of urban residents in Iran had access to treated water and sewage hookups in their homes. Today, that number is almost 100 percent for urban areas, though only about 87 percent of rural homes have access to water and sewage lines.

Rainfall is uneven in Iran, which leads to water shortages in some areas. The rain is also highly seasonal, and some areas receive their entire year's rainfall in a few days. To even out the water supply across the nation, Iran envisions building a network of **desalination** plants and pipes to deliver the drinkable water throughout the country.

Shelter

After the national census of 1966 found that about a third of Iranian "households" didn't have a house, the government created a housing department to deal with the issue. Many families doubled up in homes, whereas others were homeless. The effort to build affordable housing began before the Islamic Revolution and continued in the postrevolutionary period. The new government made a priority of building affordable housing. This allowed multigenerational families who had been living under one roof to have separate places of residence. By the 1990s, the average house contained 1.14 households rather than 1.5.

A traditional home in the town of Masuleh.

Abyaneh is one of the most historic villages in Iran.

Former president Mahmoud Ahmadinejad began an ambitious housing project in the late 2000s that resulted in a devastating unintended consequence for the price of housing in Iran. Because of the way the plan was implemented—including poorly conceived funding, structural and engineering problems, and instances of corruption—it ended up delivering not an influx of affordable housing but skyrocketing prices and unfinished projects sitting and decaying to the current day.

Personal Safety

Violent crime levels in Iran are considered moderate. That said, those crimes occur not only because of things like robbery but also because of corruption and political terror. In contrast to other cities, residents of Tehran report that they are more afraid of violent street crime occurring during daylight hours than nighttime hours. The murder rate in Iran is about half that of the United States.

Violence is an old part of Iranian politics. The shah of Iran used gang leaders to maintain order on the streets of Iran. The Rashidian brothers and the Zahedi gang were two street gangs that worked

Tehran police officers patrol the streets on motorcycle.

The Zahedi gang was named after a former government official. Pictured here, Ardeshir Zahedi sits with President Nixon in Tehran.

with the shah's secret police. The Zahedi gang is named after former general Ardeshir Zahedi, who was the government official in charge of the coup against democratically elected Prime Minister Mohammad Mosaddegh in 1953.

The Iranian Revolutionary Guard has also been known to use violence. The Guard works with both Shi'a and Sunni street gangs to subvert anti-government protests. Some criminal organizations like Jundallah, a narcotics gang, have a political anti-government front but operate primarily for profit.

Personal Well-Being

Most countries hold the opinion that it is in the interest of government to maintain some common, basic standards about education, technology access, health care, and the environment. Such standards protect against calamities that can befall a society, such as epidemics, environmental disasters, and segments of society getting left behind.

Iran is a mixed bag of intention and consequence. The government states wonderful intentions for the betterment of its people, but the follow-through has led to success with some projects and embarrassing failure with others.

Education

Iran has a K–12 education system that begins at six years old. The first eight years of education are mandatory. The last three are optional. Higher education is available to those who achieve a high school diploma and pass an entrance exam. Many young people are not granted a chance at higher education because many families make their children leave school after eighth grade, sometimes younger. Poverty is such a threat in Iran that many children must go to work as young as 10 to help support their families.

A group of Iranian schoolgirls.

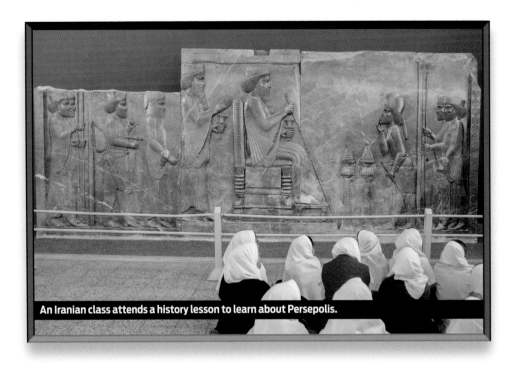

An Iranian class attends a history lesson to learn about Persepolis.

Information Access

Almost two out of every three Iranians have Internet access. People began adopting the Internet rapidly after the year 2000. As of 2012, around a quarter of all Internet sites were blocked in Iran by government censors. Uprisings in 2013 led to half of all sites being blocked, including all major social media sites like YouTube, Facebook, and Twitter. Many online journalists face harassment.

Freedom of expression is protected by the Iranian constitution, with one exception: Expression that violates Islamic principles is illegal. That can include many different things. Authorities will use this exception as an excuse to limit press freedom. As of the end of 2016, eight journalists were serving prison sentences because of their work. Communications, including SMS texts, are monitored by authorities for anti-Islamic expression.

Mobile phones and devices have penetrated as deeply into Iranian society as anywhere else. There are more mobile phone numbers in operation than there are people in the country. Landlines lag behind at 37 lines per 100 people.

Internet access is pretty easy to come by in Iran. Iranians may use their mobile devices on mass transit to access social media sites.

Whether they are young or old, many in Iran use cell phones.

Health and Wellness

The average life expectancy in Iran is 71.4 years old. This has gone up 1.4 years since the year 2000. This is slightly higher than the UN global average of 70.5 years. Just over 4 percent of economic output goes to health care. Thirty thousand tourists visit Iran each year to receive health care. The typical health tourist comes from a neighboring country like Iraq or Pakistan.

Environment

Iran's top environmental challenge is reducing air pollution in cities. The capital, Tehran, is one of the most polluted cities in the world. The World Bank estimates that Iran loses $640 million a year due to air pollution–related deaths. This means that the potential **productivity** had these deaths not happened is valued at $640 million.

Recent policy for public transport will lead to the replacement of aging gasoline-powered buses with natural gas–powered ones. However, in 2018, most cars in Iran ran on leaded gas instead of unleaded. Emission controls for cars are unavailable because of international sanctions.

Air pollution over the Tehran skyline.

Rapid development of oil drilling in the Caspian Sea has caused environmental difficulties in that area. Local aquatic life has been harmed by oil and chemical spills. Pipeline construction from the sea has contributed to deforestation in the region. One official said of overall tree destruction across the country, "In a matter of 100 years there will be no trees left in Iran if the devastation continues at such a pace." Iran has chosen undersea construction plans for a major pipeline between Iran and India.

Opportunity

Generally, people who grow up in Western democracies view themselves as having a lot of autonomy in the choices they make for what they do for work, where they live, and who their friends are. Freedom to choose what work one does is not guaranteed to everyone in the world. Western governments don't get into the business of assigning work to their citizens. But that isn't the case everywhere.

Countries like North Korea and Venezuela choose what work their people do. Iran doesn't fall into the same category of "work dictator" as these countries; however, social, religious, and economic obstacles make navigating work and other life necessities a minefield. The requirement that all laws and government actions must conform to Islamic law can severely limit freedom of expression in areas such as the work that people do, how they speak about their government, and what they can say on social media.

Personal and Political Rights

Iran has been criticized for its human rights policies by a number of groups both inside and outside of Iran, including the United Nations. Critics point to the restrictions Iran's government places on freedoms and the punishments inflicted for violations of those restrictions. Laws against sex outside of marriage and homosexuality can include years of imprisonment. Punishments for some violations can include execution, even if the guilty party is under 18 years of age. Prisoners as young as 15 years old have been executed. Although Iran tolerates some Christian and Jewish communities, the government has come down hard in persecuting other faiths, like the Baha'i religion.

Several organizations have protested the treatment of persons in Iran, from those who are being treated with violence while incarcerated to the LGBTQ community.

Learn about
Iran's distressing
penal practices.

Instagram Models Rounded Up for Immoral Posts

In the summer of 2018, in a port city 630 miles from the Iranian capital of Tehran, a roundup of Instagram models who crossed a legal line took place. About 40 people were arrested in the city of Bandar Abbas. Their crime? Corrupting the morality of Iranian society by wearing too short of a dress or too modern of a haircut in their Instagram posts. Their punishment? Staying in prison until they made a "confession" video saying they were sorry for their acts and that they had learned their lesson.

One popular Instagram star made a video saying that she didn't mean to break Iranian cultural norms, but that she made the videos solely to get more followers. It's unknown if she made the video because of pressure from police. Another model said in court, "All people love beauty and fame. They would like to be seen, but it is important to know what price they will pay to be seen."

Many Iranian women who never before posted to social media protested the arrests by making reaction videos of themselves dancing in Western clothes. Police said they would crack down further. However, the number of reaction videos became so voluminous that police resources were challenged. In fact, the Iranian government has turned to Kim Kardashian as the scapegoat.

According to the Iranian Revolutionary Guard, Kardashian is a spy on a mission to corrupt young people away from Islam by posting immoral photos on Instagram. Perhaps the Iranian government figures a scapegoat will be more effective at getting people to stop posting colorful photos to social media and less trouble than rounding up women who like showing off in Western clothes.

Freedom of Choice

Abortion was opened up in the final years of the shah's rule as a way to demonstrate that the monarchy of Iran was moving toward a modern society. The act legalizing abortion didn't last long, though. The 1978 law making abortions an option was reversed by the Ayatollah Khomeini after the 1979 revolution.

Abortion is seen as *haram* under Islamic law. *Haram* is the word for things that the Qu'ran and other Islamic sources say are forbidden to followers of Islam. Although terminating a pregnancy in and of itself isn't mentioned in the Qu'ran or other religious writings used in Sharia law, the sanctity of life in general is mentioned frequently. This has been used by religious scholars as an argument against abortion. In contrast, the Qu'ran has several passages that mention the importance of the health of females. This has allowed loopholes to emerge that allow for abortion if the health of the mother is threatened or if her ability to care for the child is compromised because of a genetic disease.

Tolerance and Inclusion

Iran has one of the world's most bizarre policies on LGBTQ rights. Homosexuality is illegal in Iran and considered a capital sin in the government's view of Islam. This means that someone who is gay can be put to death. However, as with drug addiction, the government gives gay people the option of therapy. In the case of Iranian law, this therapy involves changing one's gender: Gay men are pressured to undergo gender reassignment surgery and become females, and vice versa. The state medical system pays for therapy and treatment on an income-based sliding scale. Powerful clerics have the view that although homosexuality is a capital sin, the reason for an individual's sexual preference can be due to that individual being trapped in the wrong body.

Higher Education

Even though Iran has a network of universities, much of the educated workforce sits waiting for political progress. The country is at a standstill as sanctions disrupt important projects. For example, an education offered at one of the country's top engineering schools could be put to use on constructing roads, bridges, buildings, and farms. Instead, lots of educated adults sit idle.

That said, Iran has an impressive university system. The need for government to expand higher education and make it more available to the people is written into the Iranian constitution. The fact that world-renowned schools date back to the Zoroastrian era shows that throughout history Iran has seen an educated population as a way to prosperity. (Zoroastrianism was Iran's prevailing religion until the rise of Islam.) Around the time of Islam's founding during the sixth and seventh centuries CE, the Academy of Gondishapur was the most important medical school in the world. The first modern medical school in Iran was founded at Urmia University by an American missionary named Joseph Cochran. The school opened in 1878 and continues teaching medicine today.

University students sit with their teacher and draw during an art lesson.

Text-Dependent Questions

1. True or false: Abortion is illegal in Iran under all circumstances.

2. What recent environmental challenges have been caused by oil drilling?

3. Explain how the Iranian government treats those accused of homosexuality.

Research Project

Research the cultural and intellectual contributions of Persia and Iran throughout the ages. What are some significant achi evements, and how did they impact Western culture? Write a brief report summarizing your findings. Bonus: Create an annotated time line to illustrate these achievements, with information about key figures, academies or schools, and other information.

Society and Culture

Despite its strong theocratic government, Iran remains a diverse country with many ethnic groups and spoken languages. Its roots in the culture of Persia, one of the oldest in the world, gives its literature, food, and architecture a distinctive character and its people a link to the past.

Iran's Population

The birth rate in Iran is 17.9 per 1,000 people, whereas the death rate is 5.3 per 1,000 people. This means that in a single year, there are almost 18 new people born for every 1,000 people living. The death rate shows that a little over five people per 1,000 die in a single year. Over 75 percent of couples use some form of **contraceptive**. Islamic teachings generally approve of contraception for family planning.

Iran loses only one person per year to a foreign country for every 5,000 people. The country restricts international travel for those it deems a security risk. Journalists, activists, and others who

Words to Understand

Colonization: The process of occupying land and controlling a native population.

Contraceptives: Devices or drugs intended to prevent pregnancy.

Indigenous: Something, such as people, plants, or animals, that has occupied a space for an extended period of time.

The ancient village of Abyaneh still holds on to traditional Persian culture.

Iran's Society and Culture at a Glance

Population	82,021,564
Population Rank	17
Sex Ratio	1.03 males/females
Age Distribution	24.19 percent age 0–14; 14.69 percent age 15–24; 48.57 percent age 25–54; 7.22 percent age 55–64; 5.32 percent age 65 and over
Ethnic Groups	Persian, Azeri, Kurd, Lur, Baloch, Arab, Turkmen, and Turkic tribes
Religions	Muslim (official), 99.4 percent; also small minority religions such as Zoroastrian, Jewish, Christian, and unspecified, 0.6 percent
Languages	Farsi, Azeri Turkic and Turkic dialects, Kurdish, Gilaki and Mazandarani, Luri, Balochi, Arabic

It is extremely difficult to obtain a visa or passport to leave the country of Iran.

speak out against the government have their passports restricted, a practice that leaves Iran with a very low migration rate.

The majority of Iranians are under 35 years old. The largest concentration of people falls between 15 and 35, mainly because of the Iran-Iraq War. The war had a devastating effect on Iran's young generation at the time. The loss of life was so great that after the war the Iranian government pressured families to have lots of children. That postwar generation now represents the largest segment of Iran's population.

Religions

Iran is a theocratic state whose official religion is Shi'a Islam. Shi'ites make up 90 percent of the country's population. Another 9 percent belong to the Sunni Islam sect. Other religions in Iran include a small percentage of Zoroastrians, Jews, Christians, and other religions. Zoroastrians, Jews, and Christians are the only non-Islamic religious groups that are afforded legal protections. Outside of Israel, Iran has the Middle East's second-largest Jewish population at around 8,500; Turkey has the largest with around 15,000.

The Schism within Islam

The Shi'a and Sunni sects of Islam came into existence shortly after the death of the prophet Muhammad, the founder of Islam, and both of them have been in conflict with each other since their origins.

At the heart of the conflict is a debate over who was the rightful heir to the prophet Muhammad. The Shi'a believe it was the prophet's son-in-law, Ali, whereas the Sunnis believe leaders emerge from a commonly held tradition. Other differences between the two sects include varying interpretations of Muhammad's sayings, what the end of the world will look like, and the eventual return of the Twelfth Imam, a sort of Islamic savior figure.

The two groups have not been fighting or mistreating each other throughout the entirety of the last 1,500 years, however. Today's animosity began at the end of World War I when parts of the Arab world started embracing nationalism. Seeing nationalism as a secular influence at odds with Islamic teaching, adherents to more extreme interpretations of both Shi'a and Sunni Islam started actively recruiting followers.

By the 1980s, those followers had helped establish a monarchic and theocratic Sunni-based state in Saudi Arabia and a theocratic Shi'a-based one in Iran. Fifty years of each group using the other as a political punching bag to stoke the passions of their own groups have led to lots of hatred on each side. Similarly, each side blames the other for mistreatment in countries where one or the other are in the minority. This generally comes from Shi'ites in Saudi Arabia complaining about mistreatment from the Sunni government, whereas in Iran, Sunnis complain about ill treatment they receive from the Shi'a government.

The most prominent modern conflict between the two branches of Islam is the Iran–Saudi Arabia proxy conflict. Since the Iranian Islamic Revolution, the two countries have been trying to gain influence in the region. The focus of today's problems began during the Arab Spring of 2010. Protests began in Tunisia and spread throughout most of the Middle East. The spring of 2011 saw people from all walks of life go into the streets of major cities demanding more freedom.

In response to potential threats of unrest within its own cities, Saudi Arabia wished to form a Gulf Union encompassing most Middle Eastern states. The particulars of what the union would look like or how it would work were never formalized. The idea was immediately rejected by every other country in the region save for Bahrain. Still, the proposal itself scared Iran, fearing any potential, or even suggested, increase in Saudi Arabian influence.

Each side began to take economic and political shots at each other and any allies nearby. The tit-for-tat relationship culminated in January of 2016 when a Shi'ite cleric was put to death in Saudi Arabia on unsupported charges of taking up arms against the Saudi government. His execution brought street protests to Iran that resulted in the burning of the Saudi Arabian embassy in Tehran and the severing of diplomatic ties between Iran and Saudi Arabia. Later that same year, Iran banned travel to the Hajj, an annual pilgrimage and major religious event for all of Islam that is held in Mecca, Saudi Arabia. The ban lasted only one year, and pilgrimages were allowed to resume in 2017.

IN THE NEWS

Iranian Suspended from Important Religious Pilgrimage

One man giveth, another can taketh away. That's how one of Islam's most sacred traditions was handled in Iran due to a dispute with Saudi Arabia. The supreme leader stopped all religious pilgrimages to Mecca in 2016. This was a major disruption in the lives of thousands of Iranians. Among the things that a follower of Islam must do is make a pilgrimage to Mecca at least once in his or her life. This pilgrimage is called the *Hajj*, and it happens each summer. Millions of people make the journey each year. In 2016, Ayatollah Khamenei suspended all Iranian travel for the Hajj over the execution of a Shi'ite cleric in Saudi Arabia. Pilgrimages were allowed the following year. However, diplomatic tensions with Saudi Arabia remain high, and the Iranian government has said that the supreme leader reserves the right to suspend future pilgrimages.

Ethnic Groups

Iran has several **indigenous** ethnic groups that have continuously lived for thousands of years within at least part of what today makes up the Iranian nation. The two major ethnic groups in Iran are Iranic and Turkic peoples. Each group has a number of subgroups. The majority of Iranic peoples are Persian and Kurdish, with minority groups such as Mazandaranis, Gilakis, Tats, Talysh, Baloch, and Lurs. The Turkic groups consist of Azerbaijanis, Turkmen, and Qashqai. Here are some brief histories of each.

- **Persians** are an ancient branch of nomadic tribes found 3,000 years ago throughout what is now Iran and neighboring countries. The first permanent settlements appeared in the central plains of Iran around the tenth century BCE Persians make up over half of the Iranian population and largely practice Shi'a Islam.

- **Kurds** originate from the same Iranian nomadic tribes as Persians, settling in the mountainous areas of what is now northern Iran, Iraq, and southern Turkey. They have their own language branches, which differ as greatly from one another as do English and German, and customs that differ from Persian traditions. The Kurds also use a different legal code. Instead of Sharia, they use an interpretation of Islamic law called Shaf'i. Shaf'i gives less weight to the thoughts of scholars than does Sharia. Kurdish society today is very modern. Most Kurds want an independent Kurdistan out of Kurdish-populated territories in Iran, Iraq, and Turkey.

- **Mazandaranis** are one of a number of ethnic groups that settled around the Caspian Sea; their genetic history aligns them more to Georgian and other European groups. The majority of Mazandaranis practice Shi'a Islam.

- **Gilakis** are closely related to the Mazandaranis. They are also found along the Caspian Sea, and their languages and customs are very similar. The major distinction between the two groups is the greater Persian lineage of the Gilakis, mainly through female lines likely introduced as part of ancient military conquests of surrounding Persian tribes. Gilakis culture prizes farming. This makes them some of the most knowledgeable and successful farmers in Iran.

- **Tats** are an ethnic group in northern Iran. Most of the country's followers of Zoroastrianism and Judaism come from this ethnic group. Even today, most Tats are involved in farming, though a sizable population that has been integrated into city life live in the suburbs of Iran.

- **Talysh** is another group in the Caspian Sea area. Their presence predates other groups, and they have their own language with northern and southern dialects.

- **Baloch** peoples originated in Syria. They migrated across the Middle East over hundreds of years to settle in the southeasternmost part of what is now Iran around the ninth century CE.

- **Lurs** are a group who come from the oldest tribes to have lived in parts of Iran. They largely mixed with the Kurdish

A Baloch woman shopping for clothing in a market.

population and have been grouped in with Kurds at different times in history. Today they have their own culture and language. Their presence is heaviest is southwestern Iran.

- *Azerbaijanis* are one of several Turkic ethnic groups who live in Iran. They migrated from Azerbaijan to the area of northern Iran in the eighth century BCE. Soviet troops occupied Iran's Azerbaijani territory to secure supply routes during World War II.

- *Turkmen* have a number of small communities in Iran. Turkmenistan was one of the old Soviet republics that gained independence in the early 1990s. The origin of the Turkmen people comes from a mixture of Turks who migrated to the area around 1,000 years ago and local Iranian tribes already present in the area. Turkmen in today's Iran are seminomadic. Cattle breeding is their main industry.

Turkmen women and children dressed in traditional garb.

- *Qashqai* are descended from the nomadic tribes of central and southern Iran. They are primarily of Turkish origin, with the influence of other groups added from centuries of wandering. Today, some members of this group are still nomadic, though many have settled around the cities of Shiraz and Firuzabad. Since the 1960s Iranian authorities have been building sedentary communities for the Qashqai. They are the traditional rug makers of Persia, and influencing them to settle in permanent communities promotes increased production of a small but significant Persian export.

Languages

Iran officially recognizes two languages: Farsi and Arabic. Farsi is used for all governmental writing, such as laws and reports. Arabic is the recognized language of Islam within Iran. All religious writings are done in Arabic. Both Farsi and Arabic are taught in schools.

A Father and his children in a Qashqai settlement.

A small Qashqai settlement.

Other languages are common among minority ethnic groups. Azerbaijani, Kurdish, Gilaki, Luri, and Balochi are some of the minority languages spoken in Iran. Local and ethnic newspapers may publish in their own native language. Schools may teach using those languages, too, but Persian and Arabic must still be taught. Funding to teach minority languages in schools must come from the local community and not the education ministry.

Foods

When empires rise, one of the biggest impacts they have on cultures around them is their food. Iranian food is most widely known as "Persian cuisine" around the world. Persian influences can be found in Greek, Russian, Indian, and Chinese food.

The typical Iranian diet consists of combinations of meat, rice, vegetables, and nuts. Many different spices are used in Persian cuisine, including saffron, cardamom, and hogweed. Unique condiments made from herbs and nuts, including tahini sauce and delar, are found on Iranian dining tables.

A family gathers for a picnic at a park in Tehran.

A man and woman prepare a traditional Persian dish, dolmeh—stuffed grape leaves.

Nuts and vegetables play a big part in Iranian diets. Nuts are one of Iran's significant export products after oil. Many dishes are made with butter from almonds as well as other nuts. A rice pudding made with saffron, called sholezard, is one of the most popular desserts.

National Holidays

Iran has more national holidays than any other country in the world. Twenty-five days a year are spent outside of work and school celebrating a civil or religious holiday. Nowruz is the Persian New Year celebration. The first day of the year in the Iranian calendar is the first day of spring, so Nowruz falls around the time of the spring equinox, between March 21st and 24th. Norwuz is celebrated by what Iranians call "shaking the house." This is colorful way of describing what is similar to "spring cleaning" in the United States. People clean their homes, shop, and prepare for four days of parties full of traditional food and dance.

The anniversary of the Islamic Revolution on February 11th celebrates the end of street battles between supporters of the

A street vendor sells various spices and nuts.

Growing wheatgrass is a tradition followed by those who celebrate Nowruz.

*Learn more
about Nowruz.*

Ayatollah Khomeini and supporters of the shah. The official police were defeated in the battle and eventually joined the revolution. This is the day that Khomeini became the official leader of Iran. The day is celebrated with rallies and remembrances of the Islamic Revolution.

Iranians celebrate the anniversary of the Islamic Revolution each year.

It may seem strange to have a day celebrating the government takeover of a country's oil industry. But this government act passed in 1951 is seen as Iran's declaration of independence. British and American businesses had built and owned much of the Iranian oil industry. Taking the industry away from these companies was for Iranians a means of breaking loose from **colonization**. The anniversary is celebrated every year on March 20th.

Other major holidays include Islamic Republic Day (March 30th), which marks the founding of the Islamic Republic of Iran. The day is honored through rallies and other patriotic observances throughout the nation. Sizdah Be-dar (March 31st) is the day after the Islamic Republic Day. The name translates to "nature day," and it's spent outdoors with friends at large community picnics. Demise of Imam Khomeini (Khordad 14/June 4th) honors the death of the first supreme leader, Ayatollah Khomeini. The day is reserved for solemn religious observances. Finally, Revolt of Khordad 15 (Khordad 15/June 5th) is a remembrance of protests begun on this day in 1963 over the jailing of Ayatollah Khomeini.

A Dispatch from the Revolution

During Ayatollah Khomeini's political imprisonment in 1963, the shah very seriously considered having him put to death. His crime? Insulting the shah. The head of the shah's secret police, Hassan Pakravan, pleaded with the shah to spare Khomeini's life. The chief spy felt that executing the Ayatollah would only result in protests. So, the shah spared Khomeini's life, and eventually he was freed. After the revolution, Ayatollah Khomeini ordered Pakravan—the man who had saved his life—put to death. A confidant of Khomeini's argued for sparing Pakravan's life and pointed out to the supreme leader that Pakravan had persuaded the shah to spare him. The ayatollah's response was, "He should not have."

Crowds of people picnic outdoors during Sizdah Be-dar—"nature day."

Text-Dependent Questions

1. What are Iran's two major ethnic groups?

2. Name two religions in Iran other than Islam.

3. True or false: Iran has more holidays than any other country.

Research Project

Research two cities in Iran that do not include the capital of Tehran. Find out about their histories, key events, predominant ethnic groups and languages, and cultural landmarks. Pretend you are a travel guide, and write a summary for your tour group comparing and contrasting the two cities and their relationship to Iran as a whole.

Series Glossary of Key Terms

Absolute monarchy: A form of government led by a single individual, usually called a king or a queen, who has control over all aspects of government and whose authority cannot be challenged.

Amendment: A change to a nation's constitution or political process, sometimes major and sometimes minor.

Arable: Describing land that is capable of being used for agriculture.

Asylum: When a nation grants protection to a refugee or immigrant who has been persecuted in his or her own country.

Austerity: Governmental policies that include spending cuts, tax increases, or a combination of the two, with the aim of reducing budget deficits.

Authoritarianism: Governmental structure in which all citizens must follow the commands of the reigning authority, with few or no rights of their own.

Autocracy: Ruling regime in which the leader has absolute power.

Bicameral: A legislative body structured into two branches or chambers.

Bilateral: Something that involves two nations or parties.

Bloc: A group of countries or parties with similar aims and purposes.

Cash crop: Agriculture meant to be sold directly for profit rather than consumed.

Central bank: A government-authorized bank whose purpose is to provide money to retail, commercial, investment, and other banks.

Cleric: A general term for a religious leader such as a priest or imam.

Coalition force: A force made up of military elements from nations that have created a temporary alliance for a specific purpose.

Colonization: The process of occupying land and controlling a native population.

Commodities: Raw products of agriculture or mining, such as corn or precious metals, that can be bought and sold on the market.

Communism: An economic and political system where all property is held in common; a form of government in which a one-party state controls the means of production and distribution of resources.

Conscription: Compulsory enlistment into state service, usually the military.

Constituency: A body of voters in a specific area who elect a representative to a legislative body.

Constitution: A written document or unwritten set of traditions that outline the powers, responsibilities, and limitations of a government.

Coup: A quick change in government leadership without a legal basis, most often by violent means.

De-escalation: Reduction or elimination of armed hostilities in a war zone, often directed by a cease-fire or truce.

Defector: A citizen who flees his or her country, often out of fear of oppression or punishment, to start a life in another country.

Demilitarized zone: An area where military personnel, installations, and related activities are prohibited.

Depose: The act of removing a head of government through force, intimidation, and/or manipulation.

Détente: An easing of hostility or strained relations, particularly between countries.

Developing nation: A nation that does not have the social or physical infrastructure necessary to provide a modern standard of living to its middle- and working-class population.

Diaspora: The members of a community that spread out into the wider world, sometimes assimilating to new cultures and sometimes retaining most or all of their original culture.

Diktat: An order from an authority given without popular approval.

Disenfranchise: To take away someone's rights.

Displaced persons: Persons who are forced to leave their home country or a region of their country due to war, persecution, or natural disasters.

Economic boom: A period of rapid economic and financial growth, resulting in greater wealth and more purchasing power.

Economic reserves: Currency, usually in the form of gold, used to support the paper money distributed through an economy, available to be used by a government when its own currency does not have enough value.

Edict: A proclamation by a person in authority that functions the same as a law.

Embargo: An official ban on trade.

Federation: A country formed by separate states with a central government that manages national and international affairs, but control over local matters is retained by individual states.

Food insecurity: Being without reliable access to nutritious food at an affordable price and in sufficient quantity.

Free-floating currency: A currency whose value is determined by the free market, changing according to supply and demand for that currency.

Fundamentalist: A political and/or religious ideology based explicitly on traditional orthodox concepts, with rejection of modern values.

Gross Domestic Product (GDP): The total value of goods and services a country produces in a given time frame.

Hegemony: Dominance of one nation over others.

Heretical: When someone's beliefs contradict an orthodox religion.

Indigenous: Referring to a person or group native to a particular place.

Industrialization: The transition from an agricultural economy to a manufacturing economy.

Inflation: A general increase in prices and a decrease in the purchasing value of money.

Insurgency: An organized movement aimed at overthrowing or destroying a government.

Islamist: A military or political organization that believes in the fundamentals of Islam as the guiding principle, rather than secular law; often used synonymously (although not always accurately) with Islamic terrorism.

Jihad: A struggle or exertion on behalf of Islam, sometimes through armed conflict.

Judiciary: A network of courts within a society and their relationship to each other.

Mercantilism: A historical economic theory that focuses on the trade of raw materials from a colony to the mother country, and of manufactured goods from the mother country to the colony, for the profit of the mother country.

Migrant: A person who moves from place to place, either by choice or due to warfare or other economic, political, or environmental crises.

Militia: A group of volunteer soldiers who do not fight with a military full-time.

Municipal elections: Elections held for office on the local level, such as town, city, or county.

Nationalize: When an industry or sector of the economy is totally owned and operated by the government.

Parliamentary: Governmental structure in which executive power is awarded to a cabinet of legislative body members, rather than elected by the people directly.

Paramilitary: Semimilitarized force, trained in tactics and organized by rank, but not officially part of a nation's formal military.

Patriarchy: A system of society or government in which power is held by men.

Police state: Nation in which the state closely monitors activity and harshly punishes any citizen thought to be critical of society or the government.

Populism: An approach to politics, often with authoritarian elements, that emphasizes the role of ordinary people in a society's government over that of an elite class.

Propagandist: A person who disseminates government-created communications, like TV shows and posters, that seek to directly influence and control a national audience to serve the needs of the government, sometimes employing outright falsehoods.

Proportional representation: An electoral system in which political parties gain seats in proportion to the number of votes cast for those seats.

Protectionist: Actions on behalf of a government to stem international trade in favor of helping domestic businesses and producers.

Reactionary: A person who opposes new social and economic ideas or reforms; a person who seeks a return to past forms of governance.

Referendum: A decision on a particular issue put up to a popular vote.

Refugee: A person who leaves his or her home nation, by force or by choice, to flee from war or oppression.

Reparations: Payments made to someone to make amends for wrongdoing.

Republicanism: A political philosophy of representative government in which citizens elect leaders to govern.

Rubber-stamp legislature: Legislative body with formal authority but little, if any, decision-making power and subordinate to another branch of government or political party leadership.

Sanctions: Political and/or economic punishments levied against another nation as punishment for wrongdoing.

Secretariat: A permanent administrative office or department, usually in government, and the staff of that office or department.

Sect: A subgroup of a major religion, with individual beliefs or philosophies that divide it from other subgroups of the religion.

Sovereignty: The ability of a country to rule itself.

Statute: A law created and passed by a legislative body.

Subsidies: Amounts of money that a government gives to a particular industry to help manage prices or promote social or economic policies.

Tariff: A tax or fee placed on imported or exported products.

Theocratic: Of or relating to a theocracy, a form of government that lays claim to God as the source and justification of its authority.

Totalitarian: A form of government where power is in the hands of a single person or group.

Trade deficit: The degree to which a country must buy more imports than it sells exports; can reflect economic problems as well as strong buying power.

Trade surplus: The degree to which a country can sell more exports than it purchases; can reflect economic strength as well as poor buying power.

Welfare state: A system where the government publically funds programs to ensure the health and well-being of its citizens.

Chronology of Key Events

650 BCE	Achaemenid Empire established; first Persian empire founded by Cyrus the Great, known for creating one of the first postal systems operating over a vast area.
312 BCE	Alexander the Great conquers Persia; Persia falls to Alexander's quest to expand his empire into India.
248 BCE	Parthian Empire established.
224 BCE	Sasanian Empire established.
633	The Islamic conquest of Persia begins; expansion of the Islamic faith into Persia through warfare.
651	Establishment of caliphate; first social order based on Islamic law where religion and religious leaders have direct political power.
1219	Mongol Empire invasion and conquest.
1370	Timurid Empire founded.
1501	Safavid Empire founded; beginning of modern era.
1736	Nader shah defeats Russian and Ottoman occupiers; represents the beginning of the last great period of Persian dominance in the Middle East and in world affairs.
1870	Famine kills two million Iranians.
1906	First attempt at a written, Western-style constitution.
1925	The Pahlavi Dynasty becomes the last royal dynasty; after poisoning and other killings take out a number of princes and other successors to the throne, a new family assumes power in Iran; begins a period of direct Western influence in Iran.
1941	The Last shah of Iran comes to power.
1953	U.S. and British intelligence help the shah oust a popular prime minister; Prime Minister Mosaddegh wants to nationalize oil fields and facilities owned by British and American companies; the United Kingdom and United States fight back by supporting a right-wing coup that ousts Mosaddegh and gives the shah more power.
1979	The Islamic Revolution ousts shah and establishes Islamic Republic.

1980	Iran-Iraq War; after border skirmishes over long-disputed territory intensifies, Iraq decides to attempt an invasion of Iran to kick out the new government.
1982	Iran begins using human wave attacks; looking at the possibility of an invasion of Tehran and losing the Iraq War, the Iranian army recruits citizens to charge the Iraqi army.
1989	The Islamic Republic goes through a constitutional revision, forming today's current government structure.
2002	Secret Iranian nuclear facilities disclosed; an exiled political group in France makes public secret Iranian government information on two nuclear facilities that look to be for enriching nuclear-grade uranium.
2006	The United Nations demands a halt to Iran's nuclear enrichment.
2007	Sanctions begin; Iran's failure to address UN demands leads to initial sanctions against purchasing arms; some Iranian officials have their international assets seized; sanctions grow in scope and impact over the next eight years.
2015	The Iran nuclear agreement begins a plan to end Iranian sanctions; Iranian economy begins to grow, and the stagnation that has plagued the middle class begins to energize with forward momentum.
2018	The United States pulls out of nuclear agreement; Trump administration opposition to the agreement and the Iranian refusal to renegotiate leads to the United States reimposing sanctions; Europe agrees to move forward with parts of the agreement, but in an unheard-of admonishment, the Trump administration threatens international companies that might do business with Iran.

Further Reading & Internet Resources

Books

Basmenji, Kaveh. *Tehran Blues: Youth Culture in Iran*. London: Saqi Books, 2013. An insider's look at Iran's young generation: what they want, how they think, and why they are almost in open revolt.

Karsh, Efraim. *The Iran-Iraq War 1980–1988 (Essential Histories: War and Conflict in Modern Times)*. New York: Rosen Publishing, 2008. A thorough survey of the history and impact of the Iran-Iraq War.

O'Shea, Maria. *Iran (Countries of the World)*. Milwaukee, WI: Gareth Stevens, 2000. An informative and image-filled book on the history of Iran.

Rajendra, Vijeya. *Iran (Cultures of the World)*. New York: Cavendish Square, 2014. This book covers contemporary Iranian culture, food, festivals, religion, and economic development.

Wolney, Philip. *Iran and Iraq: Religion, War, and Geopolitics (Understanding Iran)*. New York: Rosen Publishing, 2009. This book examines the history of diplomatic and military conflicts between Iran and Iraq.

Web Sites

Iran Focus. *https://www.iranfocus.com. An English-language newspaper with an Iranian perspective on Iranian, American, and global issues.*

Global Security. *https://www.globalsecurity.org. Global Security provides a detailed analysis on military and paramilitary conflicts around the world.*

Trading Economics. *https://tradingeconomics.com. A compilation of 20 million current and historical economic indicators from 196 countries.*

Freedom House. *http://freedomhouse.org. Freedom House is an international organization promoting democracy and freedom. Its Web site includes a database assessing the status of human rights in various countries.*

Human Rights Watch. *https://www.hrw.org. Human Rights Watch is one of the world's leading organizations tracking rights abuses around the world. Its Web site contains information about human rights abuses in Iran and other countries.*

Index

Author's Biography

Norm Geddis lives in Southern California, where he works as a writer, video editor, and collectibles expert. He once spent two years cataloging and appraising over one million old movie props. Previous books for Mason Crest include the World of Automobiles series. He is currently restoring the film and video content from the 1950s DuMont Television Network for the Days of DuMont channel on Roku.

Credits

Cover

Top (left to right): saeediex/Shutterstock; Alfotokunst/Dreamstime; Fotokon/Shutterstock
Middle (left to right): C. Na Songkhla/Shutterstock; Vladimir Grigorev/Dreamstime; Alireza Teimoury/Dreamstime
Bottom (left to right): Inspired By Maps/Shutterstock; Giovanni De Caro/Dreamstime; Marcin Szymczak/Shutterstock

Interior

1, Attila JANDI/Shutterstock; 6, TripDeeDee Photo/Shutterstock; 8, ChameleonsEye/Shutterstock; 9, serkan senturk/Shutterstock; 10, serkan senturk/Shutterstock; 11, Rena Schild/Shutterstock; 13, mustafagull/iStock; 14, Bluemoon 1981/Shutterstock; 17, mark reinstein/Shutterstock; 18, Rafael Ben Ari/Dreamstime; 19, Wikimedia Commons; 21, Wikimedia Commons; 22, Attila JANDI/Shutterstock; 24, Wikimedia Commons; 27, Vladimir Grigorev/Dreamstime; 29, eFesenko/Shutterstock; 31, Pahlavi Dynasty/Wikimedia Commons; 32, Johnson Babela/Wikimedia Commons; 35, BalkansCat/iStock; 37, Khamenei.ir/Wikimedia Commons; 40, Emanuele Mazzoni Photo/Shutterstock; 41, Maryam Rahmanian/UPI/Newscom; 42, Ahmad Halabisaz Xinhua News Agency/Newscom; 44, Tasnim News Agency/Wikimedia Commons; 46, Tasnim News Agency/Wikimedia Commons; 47, Chine Nouvelle/SIPA/Newscom; 50, Stanislav Sûva/Wikimedia Commons; 53, Inspired By Maps/Shutterstock; 54, Chintung Lee/Shutterstock; 56, Mohammad Reza Davoudi/Shutterstock; 57, Ozbalci/iStock; 58, Fars News Agency/Wikimedia Commons; 60, fotosaga/Shutterstock; 61, Rolf G Wackenberg/Shutterstock; 62, Emily Marie Wilson/Shutterstock; 63 (UP), Wikimedia Commons; 63 (LO), Mohsen Dabiri-e Vaziri/Wikimedia Commons; 64, Yoyok Langgeng/Shutterstock; 67, Sonia Sevilla/Wikimedia Commons; 68, Vladimir Grigorev/Dreamstime; 70, Spumador/Shutterstock; 71, Attila JANDI/Shutterstock; 72, serkan senturk/Shutterstock; 73, Wikimedia Commons; 74, Emily Marie Wilson/Shutterstock; 75, Sulozone/Dreamstime; 76 (UP), Grigorev_Vladimir/iStock; 76 (LO), Minda photos/Shutterstock; 77, Borna_Mirahmadian/Shutterstock; 79 (UP), meunierd/Shutterstock; 79 (LO), Stefan Holm/Shutterstock; 82, Radiokafka/Dreamstime; 85, Nicola Messana Photos/Shutterstock; 86, Anatolii Mazhora/Shutterstock; 90, PPI-Images/iStock; 91, velirina/Shutterstock; 92, Emily Marie Wilson/Shutterstock; 93, Attila JANDI/Shutterstock; 94 (UP), Grigorev_Vladimir/iStock; 94 (LO), Grigvoven/Shutterstock; 95, Evgeniy Fesenko/Dreamstime; 96, Chinalus/iStock; 97, Emanuele Mazzoni Photo/Shutterstock; 98, aquatarkus/Shutterstock

02/09/22